DRIZZLE POCKET

DRIZZLE POCKET

TIM ROBERTS

BLAZEVOX [BOOKS]

Published by BlazeVOX [books], publisher of
weird little books
blazevox.org

Printed in the United States of America

Thanks to the following publications in which some
of this material first appeared: *Alice Blue*, *Tarpaulin Sky
Journal*, and *Denver Quarterly*.

Book design by Tim Roberts

First Edition
ISBN: 978-1-60964-039-2

Library of Congress Control Number 2010913000

BlazeVOX [books]
303 Bedford Ave
Buffalo, NY 14216
Editor@blazevox.org

2 4 6 8 0 9 7 5 3 1

entirely for Julie

DRIZZLE POCKET

Even with this structure of feeling telling us where we were, how else to be absent of a structure of feeling, pure space commenting on what I could develop of a structure; instead it was her holding things up, yet what would you say to the other? I was thankful for what could be here, no matter what I was the quick-living, quick-breathing, quickness bird. Then, suggesting light, the other contestants, using love.

The sword, with its glint, and glinting sheath, didn't glow. There was no analysis in the sword I was given at birth. To be sacred is part of the structure I thought I believed. Into her eyes I thought I would place my belief in all. The lovely all, first one bird, then another, then speech. Then with speech it was a structure of rhythmic grief. Even the frame, door & window, returns to reed. None of us, the bewildered, account for it, but it lives. The returning lives, the sacred timing, Zing. Structure has been known to wobble, turn to wine, and multitudes who were formerly without justification turn back to real spirits, rising in their hospital beds, returning to the polls. Even the switches were happy at touch. The only thing I would say politics is about. Surgeons don't care. In the desert, there is much sun. I'm not sure what Foucault said. I know what I feel. Were space structure, what would be up? Love glows in birth, believe all speech. Seed grief, grief is a seed. Lives spring from wine, justified in their beds of touch. About sun I feel, what's up with justified grief? What's not ultimate about it? If there were any experience through which your experience did not pass, or any experience that was not your own, then the epic would start. The race commence, coalesce. We toil in this way, in the said. Since of course what's unsaid, unrequited, remaining still the leaf attached through multiple seasons to its bridge, finally the concomitant beings moving on. The leaf grows.————Seven of us, as we waited for a train, were speaking. We were speaking to each other. Even as I am concerned about the crossover. We never imagined ourselves as simple lives. Lives of intersection, which must, I am sure, proliferate like the seeds that float from one to another speaking, reception of seeds. It generates what you saw. Brick upon brick lending its weight to a locus of conversation. The halleluiah is "I am no more than that" which suddenly is mixed with words incorporated, commandeered, by a journalist in an article about elections in Eastern Europe, or, my favorite, land-use policies, always changing. There's plenty of food, even if the conversation modifies us, even with the kind of notation that pivots forward, the blend pursued is the blend never thought. Enough. Then home. Within boundaries, or stripped of them, or exposed to what was prevented, I imagine that. Without sights, then what? Monads. Bewilderment, all experience yes we have, different concepts therein. I am joining. After the meal: bread soaked in beef juice, fries soaked in beef juice, water whose surface is coated with a thin layer of highway soot. The sandy deep, even as you intermoleculate with the mundane, stays present, moreover that which is present intermoleculates with itself above, leaving you out. My question, given these instances of real happenings, is what do I sort? It's a concern over ordering, American vernacular voicing some transcendental bliss that has to do with the seven of us. Bring them back (or did you hear that?), to me, before it is over, the platform on which we waited, beyond which there were no visible sightings that influenced the lines that extended like flax or gossamer, and that could just as easily be blown back down to Earth.————This would absolutely not constitute an "off" day, even though I'm not doing much, just laying around the house. I'll lay here for hours, reading what's nearby, which is more than satisfying, since the place is filled with interesting and unread books. For hours I lay with my back relaxed and straight as I can make it. My son tells me that when people's backs hurt they have to stay in bed for a very long time. I admit that it is a mystery to me, and of course if this is a mystery there is little reason many other things shouldn't be as well. It's up to you to make your explanations, the Upanishads, Kena, dancing in circumferences around fires in the night of the perfect self. Then each element of explanation becomes another locus of mystery, another tome to be written and read. We are occupied with something else, with things like our hands folding over exposed vintage coins, or the parallax of muscle fatigue in a browning leaf, which indicates a sentence emerging from within me, within you. There are the returned seasons, all good, brought to the first level of mind. It is time then to return to resting. I don't know about the ordinary and I've told my family so. I want to understand the division of tree trunks, too. I know we'll come to an agreement, when the days have fully entered the bloodstream, which is another way of saying there's another way.————Kneeling in prayer is counting. I was like you are. Any given second, or less, was a blessing but the aggregate resembled a city, with its slow sinking, excrescence, blasts. Children will never repeat themselves. Several of us were waiting for a train. I would then need to go back to what I wrote in my journal though I'm sure there's no reference to what's battering me, which you share. Without the story of the point I am trying to make, I don't exist. It's, well, that simple. If someone were to say, "that point you were thinking of making is worthless," then antimatter, whatever. I tell my friends there's no reason to wait for an image, as if the body would relax enough to comprehend information that would change everything. If two neighbors have a fence but all they are interested in is mirrors, a serially removed divinity, then what is the problem? If you pretend to purchase something, say as an actor in a commercial, does that mean you have done a wrong? I feel like I've succeeded at the same game that made me wonder. If poetry were ornamental it would be prose. It's only in its nondecorativeness that it treats of sublimities, which are threatening and destructive, as such difficult to discover.————I saw the virgin. My this pie! Snow collects on frosted windows. I'll never go *there* again, cold windows splitting, letting in the beyond-window. One day in the grass the stuff got in, though then it was warm as pie. The grass did extend like pasta in reverse video motion. Sitting at the dictionary with friends over tea we discovered that the word "video" had been removed. Your blood began to flow. Outside a plane flew preternaturally close and each of us checked our pockets for tissues. There are forms of awareness that are too intense for small groups. Returning to the dismembered keyboard, we decide to compare *Gray's Anatomy* to what we couldn't find in the the English language. The tea was cold. We would never have time now to go outside, though that could be put off. Your name was Tabbatha. The others could not have been happier with their aureoles. It was an index finger. Turning a baby in its crib, the noise outside became a factor, yet another appearance of one of the most seminal biblical figures. Not to be outdone you were outdone repeatedly, which meant another foray, in the miasma, to the dry emporium for tiny scalpels, my favorite part of what we still had from those times. It was up to you what you wanted to do with what came your way, but I knew what would happen. There would finally be silence, which is why I've written this, baked it, so to speak.————Without taking trouble over its lasting, we shall allow, our bellies plump with nutrient, the snow to melt in the humidifier's fumes. Now the incessant drumming, fortified robes, earth-bred face paint, knee-high moccasins, cow bells, surprised looks meant to intimidate, flames calling us into them, even amid sundry arched backs, flailing arms, the roar of ceremony through a mouth. A satiate life resists this. Each friend managing a look at the next, as if to say, "What will we go back to? They have eaten the vision." Time slows into ceremony. We have tripped into the truth and now hard breezes from January to March. The hare looms. We'd rather eat the furry flesh but let's go back when the turning point arrives. Delight moves with the summer clouds, like a dog's sight. Saturday to Saturday notes are kept: somehow we'll find out. With the gentle trickle of wavelets overtop one another something longer is heard, nearly identical to a ship's engine. Bold surfers are very delicate, as Schopenhauer would admit. Instead, there's me, the culture-making stuff I've gathered about me. And there's no neglect. In the surface line sits as many as can be here. The Thanksgiving pie is still in the fridge. Have a look. My diagram indicates that thresholds & evil places double as ceremonial inventions, so your frozen stare before the cool inside air suggests the Orient, is etherizing my ability to be anywhere in the jungle, at the simultaneous birthing and longing to rest of the conceptions that have necessitated so many doctors.————My dimmed eyes in the morning lift, as if to prove mechanism. Near me a sleeping baby whose exhalations fill my lungs. I am mummified in toilet paper, I am dreamt into myself, into the questioning of mechanism. Will you be here? I look for my friends but find piles of black smoldering ash. This must have been where secrets ended, a glassed-in hovel, filled in and covered over quite some time ago. Still though, the white tendency of our ship, this room, listening, empty but for me, the cushion on which my body lay. And still though, the dark forest, from which proceed contractual obligations the histories of which will never be digested because of dream-distractions. What have I done and asked for that I am refused, rush to the shipboard white-room, the angel-enwebbed grove sounds, minotaur, birds that mention furies in their sleep? To have seen and reordered of late meant something, for us, notations on a latticework. It must be that beyond this wall, pointing toward it, is cherished otherness. It looks at the ship's side, vertical ascension from surface to air. Is there any way to guess this? Who, after the rising of dance, after incantation and tongue, could give up shards of earth until an asset changed shape? Confronted with blue, the ship extends dark blue; challenged by populace, the ship takes on an inch. Over which the communal stare: please us but let our weakness grow. To set sea, carrying me. And you've already told me this. What's left lands within the white cell like a swan, wings hugging the circumference of air, which must be tested. The camera is every line, caressed and colored. Who will do the banking? It's clear from morning's light, recovery in sight.————Situated by turns deep within a situation. Situation oh vast lake whose surface is a sentence handed down. I can't leave this. I created a technical flow, an illusory out-turning. This morning, into the dark cold air a yellow leaf made its consciousness. As soon as my coffee was hot it would lose its hold and, nothing at first, a hole of sorts, last. But something served the same purposes. A filtered need filtered through the air. What could be above? Certainly the clouds where they are refuse us.

This attitude releases me and mountain stretches of trail bodily enter me, moving inside me, beckoning for their allowance of space and time. What happens to a tree in any given season, decay, sun epochs, institution of itself from vulnerability in the litter of the forest, its injection at last to west and east, north its undoing, oh south what will I see? How often have I been in the leering clouds, monitoring as my limbs burn away and loneliness melts? I'm among you, circling the globe. We cross the circle of moon even as we bond to the human family, peopling the surface of the vast interior plateau. I would go back but of course it's only a matter of picking up what fell and placing it meditatively in a river.————You do not find the ordinary markings, the ordinary prayers tattooed across the back, but still entangled with our epitaphs, blown down. The entire world, a place of blatant oddity, more sense than your potato murals and filth, what was a poem? The suggestion of filtered vision, bland missions of something to say, a parliament of problems in a new dream-space halting, a movie that breathes the gross daily chores of slate-to-slate shifting, blankly. In one book we looked at a man occurring to himself through a dog who had destroyed him. I was happy you knew how things went. But still fear tore at me, at itself, the reason once more the surface of it, beneath being what I wanted, with indirection and relaxants that complete one's paradise. Groups of markings praise and intersect, heat and light, newsprint, coffee—getting going, thinking democratically, Geist of opposition to the mundane. Markings never questioned, since none; markings are very land or when a short life's felt through in one corner a serif defines what's here, extrapolated, any worth, what should have been accepted. For me I must have ruined the sight of leaves, our faces in direct impression, living out addition with a laugh and certainty of step. For me, the simplest surplus.————When I watch TV, I'm not sure what's happening. There's a buzzing, planes flying over a gorge. I'm not sure what's happening. Maybe this material was inappropriate for a very specific someone. The news carried news of an explosion. Few of us had ears for that, anymore. The news is the one pilot that will not bomb, or be bombed. So many did so much work for so long it's a pity. If you choose to feel pity you may continue what you're dreading doing. If you choose to, say, carry a shopping bag. If you maneuver into a queue. That's where they all arc past the bombed TV pilots, queued behind Dante's dogs. It was like no other act, this thinking we were preparing for, even without machine entrance. Teary, this coterie we never lived among. Now it was gone, the quick horizontal excursus handed to the dawn, truly embracing several missions. I then videoed the attack with a simple pivot of lamp and lens, but the tech of the combatants proved too fierce, too accurate, and missed nothing tangible, with its flames. The same cameras were implanted in serious bulletins, and budgetary increments were such that the mission won the bet. (I'm not sure we bought anything that day.) You phone to see if I had been watching. How strange. The names felt absurd, but they were incessantly reprinted. The lift of the battered souls gave them dignity, which we fumbled over before letting out squeaks. All the time they themselves made their control apparent.————Absence that hands forever and ever clench. Tips lint palms then curl under to the base of their own finger. It wasn't there. It was fortified with expensive beads. That much shows in the column of truth, sure though shorter every day. I want to include a map. I want to make a chart showing each person's age, the current president, world and local events. The question that never gets through is who is going to do the defining. It does not matter what language you are speaking. Running away from language is not the same. Always walk away. You are walking away.————Each of the solar figures led us to the same thing. No poetry but in the pursuit. If

I have given up the serious tension of corralling words into mind given up to the influence of words outside me. Take a moment for explication, which is the poem. Nothing beyond this side of my body, home base contained in the ever-decay, in the liquid shift out, in the coarse mold of outside impression, ever renewable, agreed. Its origination there is part mother, part shelter, both of little worth. Rhetorical squid signals and we seem to be together. A particularly new interior arrives in your aesthetic as well. Be gone, you solar figures what were you but the obverse, the light verse lightening me with pain that never existed since even I couldn't speak it. No rounded-off hunk of meat am I, no head atop an intellect, an unfed heart behind a mirror. Heavy deeds relinquish attribution, the bourgeois collective defines itself through me, in languageless animalistic feints, animalisms. General safeguards, the last minute of the last quarter of a fairyland game, crowds of militant hearts all peering into speed's origin like boys circling their first microscopes. Yet it remained itself, a narrative fountain whelping its recycled liquids into the chlorinated air. If you were to touch that dust, then I'd say something else. If near its edge we last met before bracketing coasts or kneeling into the fever of broken parentage, then write it. But now, volumes of prison fiction so real, I climb up to you not knowing if you offer rest. Solar sisters everywhere offering less.———None of us agreed that it was that severe. What do I run from? The speaking boiling. Neighbors ordinarily understand absolute temperatures instantly, water, tears, salivation. Worse, derivative incomes relift freight. Tornadoes swirl below. Nightly ordinances unleash angry tempers into weird tables, scented. Wigs doff increments rolling forever. Tarry, soldier, behead. Never offering uplift anymore. Tim intuits wisdom thoroughly soberly. Weeknights domestic interludes rumble familyward, terrifying solstices basically. No, or, unless all tilts inward. Waking tournament speakers. Wow dryers inch really for, takeoff series bombs. Naturally old underpants, antiquated turds, icky worms (Talal said). Why dally? Incredible rendezvous Friday. Tortured smile beginning. Nell ordered ugly Alice to interview wanderers taken surreptitiously. Westward, damned, infernal—resisted filibuster. Torn salespeople bathe. Nigh, Othello, unleash absinthe, treatment income, watershed tipsy sicko. Wait, Desdemona, insular, Fahrenheit temperatures slide back. Nasty outcountry surprise ask twice if world tournaments sell. Wide dates increase rapidly. Fortune tellers select businesses. Nine inches upward ace tourniquets, iodine, welts tilling safezones. Winds denied instead ratchet farmhands homeward, sight babble. Nitrogen, oxygen. Weekly downgrades induce raingear, fanny taffy, simple buns. Nefereti owns until armpits taste iffy; whiff this, Seminole. Worldviews describe interviews randomly, fabulous tinsel survives, Bill. Names outrun Ugandans axed tastelessly, Interpol, World Trade, serious. White docents ignore real facts, take spitting breaks. Nero obligates ubermenches a propos Taliban insurgents wondering through Sierra winters. Delayed income. Ruined fastnesses tell several boys.————How did you discover this need? Neighbors ordinarily die. Each need was a warp traveling, gaining time, garnish tea, heat bubbling. To the lips, then. Even if I could write the disparate strands. Each sentence a new word, a unit, actual words gathering little mass. Last masses little pain us. For presence? As long as we were in the same room, I could turn my shoulders so we both could see the window without also seeing each other. Only when the phone rang did I start labeling. Large, tall, suspended, situated, towering. Why say anything, just search, ok? Elements converge to make moving and say "One day." Thank the anchors for top-notch journalistic camaraderie, pointed argument never heard the like of (your skin) segue into Regis. One need is the "more than Regis." Left with criminals, grab anything in sight. Someone is required by the theater. Shapeshifting tide teaches self to souls. The plane monumentally expires up there, above the smoke stack. There are no blues at your lips, which luminously escort autobiographical and/or substituted semantics. Oh clear. The sudden downpour caught us in its dangling ode. Embarrassed, we stayed on schedule. Our interlocutors lost contact with their second thoughts awarded second chances to solipsistic peers. Lemurs lick the standard food. Tonsils have a special stick. My jelly glints with the footprints of an obverse heat source. No one I know is on bended knee. The lavatory was closed.————Some of us head for the lake. Others transcend local accomplishments. The bread will not last. Certainly. On shore, we form a partnership. It lasts longer than you do, a success. Emblazoning personal information, there is no warm bath. That's why we're here, extenuating the predigestive syntax. Rubber. Roles to play. Reductio ad absurdum in anticipation of fingery icicles. Republican strength is memorable. It explains where I am to the other things with eyes. This is not to insult you. Landscapes like babies feet across the arched surface. Before we went back, there was a rationale, documented below. The lakes' bottom is a blank placard, hosting one version of truth and earth, then another. Finally its multifarious generations exit their morsel of touchable surface and the unity falls into malaise, never believed. Let's go. We touch for hours. The multiplex is closed. Walking home, wolves' cries echo across the new backyards. We sillily punt a bottle cap into a combat zone then take off in a preplanned rush of emotion. Darn stunts. What's left to do now is the testing, great bodies of experienced coworkers kibitzing in drop-off zones. Get on with it. Why should I care about your family? I *just don't.* Now can I have my soup back, now can the doorbell indicate its teardrop across the eardrum of my hands? Plaintive positioning is an ignorant fluke, at least according to my watch. Ding dong. Yes, you heard it, lifeless water abrogating the safe darkness of the universe, its stars designating its insecurities, bunches of nightlights. Where we are purports antipodes as quickly as superconducted particles. Christmas is almost here. The tincture of the world's barbs is abreast of our protocol. My answer is that some of us made it, others not.————————Just a little poetry. A little little poetry, in the idea of honey shut up what now Mr. Something Else. You'll have to go back to that, fragments, poetic ingratitude for all we were left. At our feet. Streaming. Never could have worked. Muddlehead. This will be hard to scan. The watch base, what I felt. My hands ice packs. Head in dumpster, out of contact. Why would you be ranting on? Even if he said to I would go away anyway, I go to create a circle. My books have told everyone everything. Just a little poetry. I'll construct another. Since there is no thinking, we're shown as we are, or wearing what we can barely remember. Anyway we're "here" not harboring nearly as much lost time as we thought we were. I'd rather be a general than a secretary of defense. That finger, there, remains on the release button. It was auto-release so he looked silly. At least it took me back to that time, when I was not as equally miserable. Incorporate play and the essence of carelessness which is in fact a balance of responsibility in an unbalanced world. There, then, sing, she'll say, she'll say, she'll say. I *read* that. Fear is motive, and extend through study. There were about three people's worth of good things beyond any negatives thought up by those closest to us. The electric joins the chorus purely in its own voice.————One of the pages had its corner folded down like us but I was not yet mechanized, none of us were. Countless airfields occupied much of the state, but we did not understand the solution to that puzzle. Forward leaning, notion of notion began to disappear since the horizontal lines began instead to tilt downward, their significance deeply called into question. Then the mirrored walk we took leaned across the table and followed its desire past present appearances, into a concrete realization of the contents of its own head. I'm not sure if you can help me understand what should have happened but the wingspan I was given seems large from this passageway, where lichen populates our brown smooth surfaces, the ones thinking could barely turn over. If this or that stage were to complicate our face to face who do you think would turn a proof forward to its plateau of world containment? O'Hara seems to have proven that quirks count for surface reflection into the bowels of the planet-space emotional timbre, which burns my backside, cancels the diseases that make us who we are, once again to share the dismantling en route to open country, a fucking ripe idea. Yet, even when the king and queen disbursed the parcels of lusts, we still could not speak, only lunge off and on, green algae pointing as the current determined in every direction except toward its root, attached to a glass plateau through which other inhabitants looked. How often have I said that observation leads to nuts and bolts rapprochement with the things they've done, with signatures placed on languageless documents, some thousand miles off. But let's continue to drape our tired limbs within the confines of our assigned seats. Let's get to know each other with assurances of this tense shore-line. Best to move slowly, no damage to the so-nar.————How much of it is there? Marking a distance. A distance marking. How does the first sundered behaving not know what we've done till now? Until this morning when I didn't know you, when sides to take would appear uncared for. What's there was philosophically incomparable to my own ability to bend down and pick up the . . . Your hand could be anywhere right now. That's the trouble, right there. That's the time line, the instant of behavior, the puff of air, the gravestone, the shadow of warmth. This is the thing that was blamed, the abandonment we knew about. But resist. Her question is answered, the columns and capitals of entropy float wing-like over birthplaces and omens. Then, exhausted with the mind of blame, even letters make time without turning away, without remembering what they were. Either they were about nothing or about something. Or they were bad, futile, a waste. But didn't the bodies thrust and have just as much truth? Where the trouble is? I'm not sure that the open line of communication is still open. Oh, now I remember. The construction worker made a flock of birds available. A nosegay punctured a girl's bean. Then the poem was over. It made one last appearance then laid down its gear. They gathered their pre-Socratic fragments and headed for the hybrid. One last tear of the umbilical, one remaining canister of cat food, one avuncular guffaw on top of another bombardment tipping the balance, which in cold light could replicate as many scepters as it had alms for.————I have a busy week lined up, one open day after another. Then the plan is to sit around at home. None of this has to do with insight. It's more a roundabout infrastructure town-hall format constituency thing. Broadly speaking, we'll get somewhere. The Anglican minister felt at home, he had work to do here, face pulled down by executive searches. No one could better describe the swollen herd, though any of us could picture it by listening to the tapes, which recorded conversations about killing the one person as a kind of message to a community. I'm reminded of basalt. Their relationship included monuments to the weather. Contracts waited in the wings even before evening, a time of small children enjoying happiness. There was no difficulty but the encounters seemed to become more squalid the longer we waited to tell each other difficult hidden things best left to outside callers. But fuck. I'm not sure that's an excuse. It's great to have your time accurately quantified, since then you know more what you're in for. Then the deciduous stuff's scheduled and it's appropriate to pack it up and go home. And regarding this business about "going home," it might be the last thing we're kind of up to. That's why I'm thrown back on the weather, and whether we'll escape the recent interlinked system of storms that caught us by surprise, or whether right here the haze and static will delete the measurement process, the serious listening.————How concomitant is the open network? Are you a participant? If one is hushed, were there outside forces that created this action, or was it a form of listening imagined beforehand? Overcautious saving is a sanctum and bliss—deciding what to leave in, rearranging the portable, looking forward to completion. You are love, even while not one thing changes from day to day. A lessness you will is the spark of intellect. Brains and dreams interfere with our physic, shoot down historic actors, levy metaphors. Babies have said this and not been appreciated. Salamanders have been vividly illustrated, deemed nocturnal. Not one of the gloriously seen people has seen my gloves. Ordinary fact that parts me from my meteors. If one's foot is buried in sand, is there a chance that guidelines will belong to the hand-holders? Nestled away, law enforcement laughs but keeps up with who we are. Brought to metaphysics, they become friends. Enter captives, again levied against each other. There is nothing difficult about the nocturnal, only about the exposure. The man's exposure is concomitant to the open network and lifts tides, a mark of center stage but equal in its demented wanderings. One Moses said she would perform that service, which, thanks to our sacred abilities, knew it could take whatever natural form it liked. This early in the season, I'm not choosing to see anything. The prisoners molt into parliaments and the muddy sink ever further. Into ideas of retainment. When you see his face, his hair, his suit, his smile, you know danger, you know that somewhere a large mass has contempt. Among these answerers nothing is unusual. Any hierarchy of sensation is perhaps endowed with an equivalent quietness.————If you were stationary then there would be little of you. If I were with you then I would be in pain again. I could never count the number of manners. This form of relative ease was left to someone who knew something. This time a savior must have appeared. He thought: "This would be nice." I'm not sure what else he may have thought. If different versions of night exist, instead of just one, then life would be better because we would think. Then each version would be like a different chapter, and many of us would create egresses and loosen our chains. This is why I have made these promises. I look in my arms and find a contentless thing, a silent yelping, a mysterious presence. I look at my memoirs, what have I done? With no warning the excrescence of a scrimmage between criminals; with no holiday, beatitudes fly in my face. My god, a method of perception, once more, the flickering, the light of judgment, the winter where compassion is like a bubble of wakefulness. For our part, our changes have adjusted to each other, witnessing like privileged candidates the snow capping our house. What were her hands but possible interpreters? What factual outlook modified the generative inclination of aphids? How ineluctable was this inability, ensconced in gold leaf? The disparate elements in a blink of incomprehensible signaling. When I understand you, I feel close to you. What appears at intervals on the radio are the structurations of guidance. Gentle female voices striate the place I live. And then, pillows. Ah, let's save this. If I were to go back into character, then what I was holding before this recent series would not allow increase. Then again, it indicates itself in a blackish Sabbath.————To be bred, to the first idea that comes to you in the schoolyard, when genuine girls are signaling their intentions. Gently to scour the bleakness where valuation leads away from itself. The grape burst but its interior constituents were gravitationally pulled away from where we were holding our tongues, not thinking. I forgot that what I was thinking could wait. My ideas were wrapped up with a lost body, which when not lost was never realized. And yet, the next later train wasn't so bad, after you'd read the poems and sent me on my way, back to Creation Hut. So surely these portraits will count, in a colorful manner, and perhaps one will be framed before it fades out mysteriously from its own surfaces. There is nothing like being taken on your own terms. This first manner of approaching the title. Your agent called. He missed you on Sunday. But now we must retrieve our passes, since it's inspection time. No wonder it's been easy, we were taken care of. Everybody's bought something. Either that or they're still young. We'd even make a game of purchasing funny money and household items. We're at the "store." The outside was unreachable on the walls. "Up high." If I were to go out on the street nothing would be more real than cold pavement, or plantings, not helloes, not visits to whole new blocks. Cinnamon, the American version, in morning bun, flavored coffee. Sweet potatoes, with marshmallows and cinnamon. Pumpkin pie with just a sprinkling.————————It's not that I've been, I'm sure that I've, the psychology as if it were near, the inhuman, how did she approach the, it was bandied about by you yourself by the people. This morning one aspect of the system gave rise to a recovery in another area. Oceans of data, and who was able to continue in such a manner? To pass by strategically—you'll never be secluded, in your poetic. Only by being there at the interrogation, only for the forging voice. How many of us can say that during this time they have been most themselves? Pouring. Without success. Pouring no witnesses. No more back and forth that illustrates our understanding. It's this instance that contents us, that I can speak through. It's that respect for what he was doing that's why I love Duncan. Then the continuous flow. Does it have to be. This morning, now. Afraid of silence. To live against it? Even its nonsilent continuation of a beat, of a measure. Of what I'm worth, of what I see. My eyes are not required to reward you. Or whether, or content, or dragged into. Remove shoes, char feet, worry. Feet marred by gravel, rough cement. How live? No lives. Continuation. It aches. Absorbs itself, this reason. You have doubted yourself to a reason. Now returned to the reason. With what I see, glass falls out of windows. Part of me is . . . , but I would say that, no matter how super it is, maintaining that high vision is like holding a pose. Are we able to go then, or do we need? There is reduced. We seem to have no habit. To stay with the unhearing, just as much as the unheard. The labyrinth holds a door, mentioned by glue on a screen. Dream. I have a sense of how I'll feel tomorrow. To tell of the good. I was a "gentle person." Come to me when I don't know what to do.————No one could designate a structure. Who would have to, anyway? To look at the road and hold her hand, some dream, pressed into action. This plan was indicative. Most likely a lost hand. And when we had the fact in place, there were suddenly no more facts, the barn was open, the olfactory and the aleatory came upon an open existence. They knew each other, there were patient remembrances pressed into action. The road could lie to itself, line by line, until what needed to be meant had its own definition, herded in. But it was still able to look, still able to turn round and round like a benefactor the towers and inclines of nation-states. I am decided, looked after, begged to end and begged to begin. Then, since only now have I started, a long slant of snowdrift, or of summer, its copse its dreamy bend of night. We are the third simple light bulb. We suggest throwing fire, playing in the ring, looking for danger that no one survives. I am meant to be with you in that limber reductions uncloud my sands. I am meant to labor, even the lispers talking, then breaking free, how little could we anticipate that. A range of factions had escaped as well, getting as far as ten to the third power meters. My choice was song, but that block of rewards didn't participate. And the timing of those rewards, finally over. Whoever was there got one and our patience remained in check as if it took far longer than blending permitted. Ah, how I remember who I wanted to be. Lives, barriers, laws reducing me to tabulatures, but still, orders of astronomical distance, like signs left to say what replication understood days ago. Who would have to, anyway? Who would come to know?———Here is my breast, so able. I've carved a place for it in the deliberate undoing, a mall hovel of a life, consuming internment. And what happened to you, where did you go, alternating behind a deep reef to lie quietly on sand? Was there some reason for begging, for taking oneself out of reach? And just as existence as we know it is not exactly there, so it still is. Ho well. Eleven thousand miles an hour, either that or we have to recalculate the whole indication, a billion years or something else. It's only the most terrifying thoughts that bring the heart out. Must have been an arm holding its stereotype adjacent to streams; this human ability, that human insight. As I imagine, a double meaning, a proverbial birth or actual, face down, eyes askew. Thanks, says the world. I didn't know you were there, I didn't know what to say, I think my awful criticism and nutty verbatim simulations of law are mistaken, wrong (as they say). Avoidable the heart-fleeing, avoidable the soldiers dying, the calculus that hermetically bonded you with an antigeneration, solving its line. Emergent from discipline, from stagnant signs. Oh, that is enough. It returns to its immortal center. It castigates and announces its existence, what you decided to live in.————A crowd waiting to board a train. I am responsible, but I have no information. Each carries a wall of attunement. I'm not sure if they are attuned, through words, to something that might be a message. They look off to the moon in such a sway. Even as a shelter of discontent. What will make them feel at peace? To make something bizarre, some glory, out of this thing fed to us. What is peace for such people? To walk to the burned train, to look up and look for why they look, and if it were possible to set at ease the sense, why make fragments, superfluous, and what takes anteriority, making us shut our legs so quickly? These were my comrades, I knew them by sight. I knew them before the world led its action, the freezing fields, accessing sharp ideas. What other ideas would there have been if we had not delighted in the small instance of angular motion? If only they would have remained with the poem during this trial. If only acknowledgment were

easier, revision so that no more bent away.
Jackrabbit, positive force. They'll learn, without
silence. Revolutions of the undeniable,
steps taken, once it's dispersed. Only then did
they come to terms, light shutting down as a
function of movement, these same planets and
light closing off possibilities, attendees who
check schedules and lovers who entwine, talk-
ing dogs, luggage rolling all on its own, sena-
tors lining up, clearer in themselves than what's
last known by the travelers here.————Now
in winter realize the united mass. The fortunes
no one knows are bent are blue are gone. Cov-
ered in snow, the erotic warmth glumness like
a candle left outside all night. That sign. That
situation reminds everyone of why they came.
First, there was exposure; then there was wit-
nessing, of who came first; the lonely, sheltered
by desertions, did I say love? I never meant
love. I could look without awe or disgust, but
with curiosity, plateau of relation. The arm of
the disarmed night, which seems to be striking
again. The praise of one dragon for another.
Who could summarize what didn't want to be
said? Centuries later the said is as obvious as
could be. Centuries hence the weather will be
different, clouds much lower, cold air rising,
balloons commingling with the features of
Hell. When these messages each get out, then
count my losses, which I won't remember oth-

erwise. The true messages have to do with momentum, the lifted hydrofoil package. The storefronts are impenetrable, capsizing without significant weight. How could I know, among the drowning passengers? Do we then conclude other orders, other tides? I think I am talking but there's no use now, these poor instances of historied fact. How could those not work their wonders, bleating sheep waning in winter? That's just it, we were animals, if not pure dumb food, then bodily. Again, the heroic movements that cross my vision grow farther and farther away, and there is no possible angle of substitution. What interest would have been possible without that? No matter how far one of us travels, there it is again. Then none other of us have that certain face again.————Come back, certain symbol. Tossed, hallelujah, toss again. Strain, where you are, there is nothing now but your contentment, which you've always possessed, even in the fire, first earth fire. I have given you to a brand of rock, dark like mud but an eternity of waves withstood. This eternity in only a few days passing. So that I would remember them in remembering where I left you. And you were for no one else but me. Like this poem buried, suffering, in an exchange of air. Will your molecules come apart, will you tarnish in the tossing? How many oceans will you tra-

31

verse or will there be this one place you sit? And for my lief I'll come back to look for you, to look for me, to seek this genuine thing never guessed until now. Your power is your ability to make us think of this one thing, to put beneath me a great mark of saturation and live with it as base, my magic carpet of flat fullness. Sit alone then. I've seen through your weight. Like me, cry then. It's only them, in this momentous window of the Golden Gate, where time more than anywhere else could stand. Here it is not lost. No one sells this land. No one gathers it with its head turned back and does not collect its dying scales. I have lost you in one of the most beautiful places I know, the most protected. There is no better resting place, if not with me. As if there were me, and I will be back there, wings aflutter as the earth rushes beneath me. It fell away, like a line of verse. A swirling tide like a petty thief picked it from my person. I will survive layers of terror regretful, the wrong outfit for this funeral. Who will be there with me once the ring is removed? Who is with me now, where unceasing motion keeps me?————(*Et j'écoute longtemps tous ces chants et ces cris.*—Appollinaire.) I am warm now, the product of a predicament of predictable feeling. First impossibility: walking along the street, seeing someone cross in front of me. Now, a certain idea of commercial, what I see is only the world where things worked, more than its outline, its whole tapestry of body, bucolic scenes of music relevant and evening breezes, I cannot, as if the people across from each other knew I'd be looking bereaved, as I was. Who wanted to listen to that? Now, if we all dress warmly, if we take care, if we in our own languages give words to one another. Now if strangely carried off, by our shining experience of voting, and we, if we look at ourselves, realize that in this spot, parcel, plot, now in its inability, now its failure turned to gravel dispersing, it cannot hold us, I am afraid to know. Which is why your holding of these talons to my face, your begetting of the sonnet's last line, your strangle-hold on contemporary understanding, your hold on music's note, scene shy to me. Seems broken, but not yet, not forward enough yet, lost in whole gallons ingested now expunged now released. If I had to listen to more of you, resistance feeling like earth resisting a post foundation or anything at all that would enter it. Not until poetry again gets exhumed, oh title of titles. Not until no one cares anymore! Then, same planet, the tableau of other planets sits in front of us. We are asked to judge. Ascend east from the opera. Kind notes at least, bargains saying their justice may come. If you want to understand this, then there would be no end to our dialogue. Then what would be missing would be music, more or less.————Anterior to first thoughts, a frustration. What I knew was usually just the thing. It was a participation in myself. Just like that beginning achievement. Even if over the course of time, a shadow-life evolved. Since this is what we know. Since over time we were deprived of a network of potential moments, you and I. And my first potential moment was a crucifix that pierced me in a wide thoroughness of tapering candlelight, a structure fed to connected generations. Your own first moment, like a whale, rolled ashore with a constant inland breeze, a mysterious body that would never break. No one will miss you if you change your shift, work another field. The protection offered by the miniscule lights can be found almost anywhere. What's suffering but the habit of drifting into the capsules of anterior delight, monuments to the monuments that are taken from the aforementioned drifting and placed, stage fright and all, next to a radiant fable of letting go. Even with these bubbles augmenting the archways and smokestack vistas, our choirs complement the rest of the nighttime. Sand roots alter tenements, and I present you with a check. Your difficult fleeing was endearing tho much shaken by passion. It was in this hour that we fell together through a textbook sidebar, and told San Francisco to vote against us. To know is only worthwhile if you can clap hands. Otherwise lyrics about a duck command the city. There is nothing like a pillow warming as the sun approaches.————————Such survival meaningful, topical, sent to rest. Early on, the instructions, from a month. Even between us there was disgust, my primal moment, your boredom. We could have been channeling my heart's truth, grain of me, and there for you would have been the hour, in the room, or you in its room. The universal respondent thing. When I was only one, there was a strange fuck in the house. It was called warp of landscape, or salt cut of my eye, milky texture overrun with design. Then labor to become yourself. Afix potholders to your tenuous hosts. I support language that mirrors any day of my life. I support language of the real. Which works and has mechanical parts that seem familiar. Which captures the undue returns, which each take their character from what's gently ancient and nude. My what a wait. My how bland. My what trouble accrues as we live, as we die by implication and implication only. My subject is somewhere in the fine print. It surrounds anyone it can find, then teaches great solemnity. I'm writing because she, across from me, is supposed to be writing, or doing something with her life. To obey. To conjure, from sentience,

what she did when she arrived at the mother's
house and spoke of going to the hospital. Must
be bleeding. I, the couch, an interlocutor. Any
emotion is located on the outer layer of the
stomach, not in the heart per se. If women cry
that implies audience, if men cry that implies
turpitude. I heard these words yesterday. Ap-
pollinaire's leather halo. Now, do you under-
stand, if I could convey that, across the aisle,
soundlessly. No meaning of the heart will be
picked up or sheltered by any of the registered.
Some people will know.————I little do un-
der have them forming within larger, big plan,
escaping like air. Who sense in land of ongoing
on that removes ice and isolation, who senses
what when to tell you to go exactly now, it re-
sults, it takes over the king, relies on, smiles on
a smile larger than periphery it was capturable
in this cup of early, only nondebatable fact
group, grasp of coffee passing commuter, only
not real already this Monday often superbowl,
argued   Trouble   unread   mis-pronounced,
deeply. The children who were painted but
placed among bubbling logos, ballooning up
unnoticed dangerously close to their gums,
now I know what Target does, that is an ac-
complishment for today, unstoppable, my
knowing where to go what things look like
from there, the ability to read no more than to
purchase. Not enough heard from where was

and past outcroppings words descending back into and from being raised once nothing was built to house them. At last, beyond argument. Then I adjust perhaps allow third, communal feeling after excursion climbed, falling back seasonal yet allowing argument. Small, after a night's rest, breaking forth from the face. How did it turn out that a conclusion fell forward, a loose facade? Determined loss of function, destined light or fear. Let me not go into the iron bar conjoining let me not go which is cultural hopelessness and the same indication I was talking about in the shelter of who we were buried in. Now, now, now, beyond the everyday, only by being beyond it can we not contribute to destruction. How can I manage to make myself one thousand times that factor?————And that dreamt festival, that stove that existed there nothing destructing move from its impact then context, situation that brought it there and impeded its becoming anything else. The diamonds once again fill my pockets, a national reserve personally avertable. I should send it off to dearly loved ancestors waiting for contact. Or maneuver the benchmark past the phenomena listed in the neighborhood directory. Even broken it's possible to manufacture a viable spirit, a tingling and voiding of muscular tension, in the side of the head. Test drive, my comfort zone, back in my kitchen surviving in my selfsame position, before the large refrigerator door. Each part of the machine is missing some enabling structural gesture, not my fault. Each face etched in defunct surfaces entices laborers to deform. New blisses have import, new bicycles come in pairs. Then with your kindness orchards rise up like flotillas a good fortune, ripe zones of tiny populace jewels. And leave then, ring out the sun of portraiture until ability croaks and petitioners ride their steeds. If becoming, then holy speaking, then remittance pestering its soldiering companions. Return the call, blah into the receiver at alternate frozen delays. Life up, like sonorous increments of church seed, the baby who will grow into a great three, the whom we'll notice on the corner some day. I've been waiting to tell you that I need to go. My ears are popping.————Actual cultural changes as I've taken them down in this note to you. Even my own love of performance wins out over measurement in the celestial partaking of the rarity of functions, of murder or every billboard meant to be the sheen and decor of. Meaning has no objective and in the world apart from the solicited roots the preparations are presented to comprehension by men and women not yet destroyed. Grown up from not being men and women we find multitudes of permissions, banks full of football our reward, the guilt-introverted trophy of the cerebral literati. Oh son, if you run from me then how can I pretend to be your own declaration of rue? If we're committed, we have nowhere to do. If we're granted banter no one cares to indicate what to heed. Any possible cause of dying, like a too-much-sun calamity, is here in front of you, ruling out any formal pity. Institutional drawbacks, but there's certainly a payoff. I'll be first to admit I like the setup and that the sheaf of unaudited, unvarnished sunlight penetrating the underbridge is exactly what's responsible for the dense square of grass amid the leftover asphalt, as well as any nighttime transformation. A hidden gull-chick is now a phantom we may appreciate one day, standing on a local beach, having traveled unique listings of time zones to return to where once we thought of writing to each other. That was the source and reason of our saying this and I can I'm sure figure something else out. These hideous neighbors. Once again we're putting up with our own surroundings. Centuries worth of pall in my pocket. I assume there are no answers. Once again the philosopher is just a philosopher, hurls his chosen text against the wall. Once again in the adjectival sky a din of invectives turns the cosmos blue.————What did you think? If you have something ordinary, tell me. If organizations need to survive, who are we? What subject could have become more than the already available subject of shipping away? We did nothing when the time came. The subjects took that into account, and then when each line of value was on the tablecloth, we paid the older gentlemen and talked openly. Since the women were the subjects of the investigation we left them standing against the wall, and management came to empty the wastebaskets. Now, look at your subject, your research. Today embarkation tells the future. You could use pure sound to get your point across. Encyclopedia of impenetrable skies, the stuff in the argument of the outer layer. The bastard refused to stand still. New news of experts gained distinctions. Whole manufactures or histories of manufacture, dreamt by the sons of linemen. One day, during the same investigation.————Last night's open exchange. Thankful for that. None of the "crew" was truly aware. None of the productive little dwarves. Did you see them escape? As I was listening last night I heard doors and feet. I heard extraordinary effort. I heard sobs, then cheers. Then silence except for the ticking of the clock that has given variant information each day. [Paragraph] I'm assuming I'm in my own bed; that I've been alive while thinking of this series. Then, even if you lived through linked plovers, I could absorb silt. Handbook of matter, that is, endless case studies. Now that we're asked to inhabit disparateness, any given highlight is a barricade. An intensity, like birth, recedes like a pall of distraction, a lake of disquiet that's ever a calm morning. Blisters arise to indicate alternate activity and despite open channels what we were missing is found out. Given these resources. [Paragraph] Looking forward to pg. 323, probably four more nights will have prominence. Then the shaft of blisters is aside, modern and tranquil, jellyfish backdrop. After silence comes generosity, what you did, what I did. The capsule, the stations, the churches. The medication that resulted in policy. The sense of pride. Righteously we expunge the torn mate, such trees and their imaginary indications of futurity, a soft honey gathering pink, plenteous pistols at heights ethereal.————Please ignore the orange light, which was brought in. It's hard to gather what the reasons were. Didn't you say that already? If no one else had the orange light, then what form would it take if you yourself began it? The formulation might not even be clear, but certainly there was a shape-shifting or earth moving beneath us, as we tried to rest. Only if I were to become a tree or something equally stationary and indisputable in its craggy regenerative flesh would I treat twice of these unusual matters. As it is, there is an idea walking the streets in someone's hair, orange ends implemented before it begins to rain. I'm wary of the structure and I'm not sure who structured this. It reads like an unfamiliar galley. We play like novices on the professional field. There is no more Valentine's Day, stones are substituted for unusual toy rings. If there is enough water, I'm sure control will drift our way again. Or it could stay on the day stage. I remember when we took communion to-gether. Each passing car had stars reflected in the street in front of it. Institutional findings were chiding someone else and we warmed up close to the equation. How do you know some-thing when you don't know what changes so quickly? If I come over to your house, does it end there? It's better if we never meet. That way, airplay's a little richer, fewer experiments, appreciation of the grotesque, instead of that awful avoidance. Now at night my dreams are the same, but that doesn't mean I've given up. Whole new organizations of people who don't know anything. And with their imaginative pillars sopping wet, they get to your house talking about their little partially realized proj-ects, two lights shining on each other, when what you wanted was an open door.————En-gage, troubled blood, untracked as in drifts of thought trackable at last. The wind fights against not only you, but anyone driving with you. Drifts of snow once surrounded us, ice as far out as the housing tracts. No rewards, strange whisper that I've only heard now. If someone dies it's for a very good reason and we'll ensure they're remembered. Too many times memory dictated by people like this, we thought hey we're gone but still each day something happens, small stones, rivers continuing, at the snow line ice beginning to melt. If within me there were lines of generation, crude implements, weathered demoralization refusing to fade, what else, then in speed's subject to shuffle off? To believe, in that folded recumbent artifice of strife, the end had positive value. Hey, fuckhead, don't go crazy on me. If the media started this Just for Me brand. I feel good, now. I'd like to see someone. Are relationships possible? Even amid the already existing is potential for whole new layers. Those are the places that true things find ability, alibi, atop streams of outmoded communication. Don't worry. I'll be ok. Even amidst slavery, we get it, get it in there. I am very true. The simpler places are genuinely heard, she's over here, I'm over there. No time can adjust itself, except now when it reaches tainted silence. Just then, a word a day the footstep for me. Thankfulness, from here on, that I'll never build another thing. Abundance, as he waits out his illness, decidedly masculine uncle of influence. A

linotype whose fearsome mane is what I re-
member. I should be so grounded in rawness.
Never any thought of service, the strength of
their phantasms does not matter.————————Po-
lice manual, photos of cops, faulty unit, new
fatherhood, etc. If you engage one second and
then relinquish the hold, you thought you
looked perfect, then at least then things were
kind of in process, more than yesterday, far out
into the future. Instantly yellow entities are
like sacred advice, teaching of yarn, yellow-
jackets, perpetual Atlantis, laughing, taken
with kinships, princely wandering, testimo-
nies, weak years, altering nothing, justice
weird, baffled lovers, forgone outrage, incar-
ceration, fugitive. Abducted, barred, confined,
destroyed, enlightened, fenced, garnered, har-
bored, interred, kidnapped, monitored, or-
dered, quarantined, sentenced, taken, undone,
vetted, weakened, x-rayed. Asked, belted, col-
laborated, delighted, enlightened, favored,
guessed, hit on, instructed, jumped, known,
lusted, mounted, nibbled, opened, pried, ques-
tioned, ratified, scented, tallied, urged, valued,
wanted, x-ed out, yelled at, zoned. Only speak,
what they were saying. Only tell me now who
understood, the administrator's body of paper-
work, check boxes, office use only, address
lines, open space. For those who checked "yes,"
signatures. If through multiple languages

someone found you, follow their form of expression, to the corner store, survival. A collective of white socks the headlands, neighboring lesson plans. Last we heard each speech pattern was riddle enough, curve of hip, lay of tongue, chin's emphasis and finally the eyes, how it was impossible for them to be silent.————How would we know about that? Exactly where would we come from? Who is supposed to be leaving all these things, in the window ocean of green, the signifiers crawling up? Could it have been another citizen, sticking to his guns just outside his cell? Certain quadrants of protected waters were abandoned, and that's just it. None of the people in the room were really there, other than a mysterious fracture, which applied to me but was in the nature of anyone but me. This suited quintillions of us quite well, until the barrage, which seemed to have been slated for me but was left up in the air. Totally something beyond the spreadsheet, the number came through in free dust and puffs of cigarette smoke. There was a subject, not properly laid out. The abhorrences were vacuumed and the validator gave a speech, tallying everything but pitching light back at its source, barely comprehending several actions. I'll tell you what's wrong with that. Outside his cell, the citizen sees windows and wants oceans, terrible questions changing shape before they can be asked. But—my question—why have you run into the tired century? What scope has enthralled these barriers yet again, uselessness of fingers, toes, face, of the whole man, trying to escape in his missionary zeal. But I never saw the first episode, the one where captain crybaby regurgitates the proem. But I was full of questions (even though there's no lack of awareness). Yet again, to relieve mind, to read. That's it, the corrective salt. Get it out, of here. To be buried with the good wishes of a community of well-wishers. I have given my work to the committee.————— They could sift through the brand tokens, this way of compromising just when it wasn't needed, just when you blew into the hills with the rest of the professoriate, with the workers, with the uniformed worshippers, Germans, in their sombreros, dangling from the train, shouting to each other, just when you decided to compromise, about what to wear that day, about tickets and such, you no longer needed to, their hands growing calloused from the metal grips, their thoughts turning even then to what they had to do, in the morning, with their mothers and fathers, after they reached the small towns to which they'd purchased round-trip tickets, a gentle visit, worth more in their eyes than some kind of love, which they were leaving behind, if only for a day, still it hurt, still they wished they weren't going, still they wished they'd said something more, to the sultry women, that would have converged, oh that would have conveyed, the extraordinary trust, that was their measure of themselves, contained, first occasionally, then more and more, finally indistinguishable, in these women their companions, who even then had no significance attached to this brief absence, foray into their previous selves blackness of obscure relation to girlhood absence freedom of absence limberness foot to greenness without him without presenting without desire itself now at last he is gone and to carve, with the fingers, then hard stones in the pocket, their smooth surfaces untroubled and echoing the surface of the skull, in its hiddenness, except when a person has been for so long away that the body, following its natural course, reveals itself through a process of decay.————————I'll leave you where you stand. Our mothers did not suckle equally and we did not share the same therapist. What if I were to lose sympathy, if it were smacked out of me? How many times could that happen, before the mildew reached the tipping point, before the stills began to transmogrify, before the very idea of a morning was flippant conversation, paranoid gossip? Don't answer. For that matter, don't breathe, and don't be like them. Scenarios crush the

47

likes of us, whose new technologies bear the correctional punishments, this frame of contrition for our sins. He must have been my friend since he took this risk. Now it's impossible to remember him. Janie from Greenwich. Breathe again, oh wild animal. Community service. Terror-stricken environment of troubled teens or confinement, oh relative ease. How do we speak to one another? Let me be your answer, let new nations infiltrate the consumption and the debris. Can we term these polarities the Pleiades, or how dark the given wing of the day? To number in the . . . counting one's fingers can happen with ease, a lifetime of ease at our fingertips. If only the hypotheses weren't there. Gunmetal sky against a closed red sea. God's "she" at the end of slavery. Thanks for the "what if" instead of the "why." Looking back, as the frame of night agitates someone waking, I find a way not to judge and there are hands over every part of me, regardless of the look in my eye.————If I were to piece together a previous circumstance. The suggestion of a hovering animal, a cow in its meanderings, a saucer full of mice, tied at the tail by floss. What do you take me for, the angel for whom the visions appeared, and the porch light glowed? Tell each other—"see." Tell anything, look forward to your exercises, the cartons of sleep. We tell each other more than we know.

But you do not suggest a war. Now is the pre-
defined season in the Indian graveyard. And
even if the hurtful pieces established a thirst or
thanksgiving I might not elaborate what re-
mains.—————There's an aspect of what we
wanted to consider that has nothing to do with
the page, but takes up where liquid in space left
off. That's fortunate, that adaptability, its warm
swim over dusty surfaces, looking for resis-
tance, letting its stopping point be something
or someone else, such as the decision of birth,
to live by the land. No one told me to become
a salesman. No one peeled off $100. No one
said this bush, this flame, this silent face. If
nothing else, we get a blank page. Then the
drones look like they're worthy.—————Part
was what you *needed* to say, doors slamming
and the gyration of it doesn't matter, gyration
of nation in need, figure that out. Go to that
higher plane, where gestural awkwardness is
not first arrival but secondary, bodies of slaves
not to adjust, but to let in! How could, open-
ing with that dog barking, so many lines orig-
inate at once, from fingertips, from the great
dome that would not once push down before
the spirits escaped it. No one is permitted to
tell once what is on top of my head, no one lifts
the equation to the lakebed, no one here gen-
erates substance first and foremost, except those
lumping and mistrusted. Three miles back we

had a conversation that, remember, included each of the nocturnal rhetorics, each frustration unmounted and so poorly borne. There is little chance that this city was what surrounded us, and more likely it was meadows reproduced in desktop calendars, but still. Then, on awaking and making fun of everyone we deigned to deign to linger at the campus, classes on notionlessness broadcast to youth, noiselessly brimming with nation. Oh, why bother, a genuine refrain of purpleness in the day's middle. And the very same group let thousands of us go on and on, until our lungs clogged, the tunnel was dug, then we needed to escape this place, no time to process what happened before the awful surrender of our imprisoners. One wish that was logged in the surviving record was for other replenishment of native speakers, whether through coffee tins of rigorism or a simple illustration of the bones of the foot. Once articles were drawn up nearly all of the signers went back to their farms, which during the revolution had been supervised mostly by women!————There was a woman running down the hall. Sarcophagi, light language implying "I've got to get out of here." Just when my dangerous immediacy, my complicated embrace of an untold, now again to fall through, as if family faces attended, waited like crushed petals destined for rebirth. The idiolect, document, the increase wavering as a domino of morning light. What, again, did we come to? Did he speak of it and then we picked up his technique? When would I be boarding that ship, as unpredictable as a mood, or a metaphor? Nothing protects my feet, which you have seen and not seen at once, basking in raw maturity. Permitted to breathe, many times over, in his repetition, which was so engaging that none of my questions took root. Turn out. Into verb, structure existing footwear, betokening high skin, at least. Ansel Adams, sitting there. Abreast, close by. You don't have anything else. Retrieve like nature does, like only hold this for as long as. New, on this side, the intention was black. There was nothing more of her than what had happened to me. Fallen grace now her control. The hairdresser, not Adams. Relative life, a hard knife, unshorn and pressed against this light. All that's ever connected from my hands. To that come and I can know this rightness, let's take that for real, know this rightness. What do I need to start for? For a sample? That's what told me to participate. Segregate. How many times was I taken away from how many hidden times were hidden from hiding? Well, having let the shelter crumble. Having to know, today, order in the telling of our. Like someone showing up at your door. She could be standing there at any

point in the divulgence of this to that, of holi-
day to holiday, cycle, lord, counting actual
people. Do you need to do this with me, or can
I go off on my own? There's someone in front
of me who is an illustration.————No letters
to. See I'm fraught but then, who can predict,
unlearned, straight up, small creature, you
know what you must do. When but not now
arms of a statue misplaced after breaking, after
being found. But what did I know? I would
rather travel to us looking at each other. I knew
plenty, which was yesterday, but to care about
that! I must have seen the obscene, crusts cov-
ering me, genuine leaps back up, either on the
street or silent, against Aceh. Teach me, tame
order, pressed by gosh what not by father in-
carnations, by peril unpliant, by goat clones, by
breast image, noses full of laser light, I was
pressed pubicly as well as publicly, microphone
sewn to my ball sack. I want at broken screens
to let relax the organic yogurt, blessing long
life. Mere aspects of coming back. Mere inter-
play, foreplay, intercourse, prose poem, a Euro-
pean 220v plug. This replacement feature, cry-
ing out, looks to be the consent that was that
body I needed to realize. Then we bring the
mountain to head space, night light, requests,
limber feelings in anyone's lips, unless there
was a decision to remove them. Variant attend-
ees and confreres, suspecting each other, label-

ing the airport with high standards, I do not stand in need of sentience. I cross out attitude by contrasting one with another, leaving behind upscale grocery stores and extremely comfortable cars, small prices paid again and again. Place of learning now about the storm's eye and about leveraging real estate, about your bag full of diapers. Anger and abruptness collude as they coterminate, through soft words. How many lexicons? Bridle not against last ideas, anything moved was signed off on. To be ashore after having been ashore forever, one's required to pardon a reminder of it.————I ask her to identify it, the dull. Certain sections, all that was granted. Ever instructable, they coaligned before agreeing on separate crimes. It was merely how I learned to speak. What events could here substantiate the strange garnish? Or how to prevent the complaints going out across the desk. Anyone I meet is love, love, love, well, possibly only an angle toward love, but still worth writing about. If only she weren't so dull, if only my propensity weren't to fathom that dullness, my own therapeutic, my sentence structure. One day we'll get married. I'll know about everything that led to this and I'll trace the archways of her physique. What a bracing periphery of nonsequitors. Not that I'm trying to hide a damn but to get something across. My mother, what a dreamt intention. And again, it's all we can do. The log wherein each sentence even identically repeated is recorded. To jump to this duty, and to hold your own actions. There were levels of advice that it should be noted were not followable to starting points. Then we participated. I read that work but ended up with a blue hypothesis, both in form and feeling. If you look at me dully I know myself. My turning reaches down my leg, to a locus of tension created by letters arriving. None of the heated family members enjoyed the platoon but love and revealing continued beyond our financial neighborhood. And why would they resist this topic? There were too many people who didn't need the people speaking. They would, for instance, conduct a campaign together, but a night alone in a house as different as a handful of cash from a dead hand. The dead should remain dead and stop trying to be alive, stop thinking they're Paris Hilton, who is me in my days of sharp wit.————Positions face in the face constellation impossible. This was my one thought, paramount to saying my one person, who would follow me everywhere. A conjunction of faces in a city park, experimental with a graveside manner, counting over and over, one, two, three. Even in the extreme it was a half parchment, even right there in the bell tower with the officials and representatives. Generals could stand there, counting everyone. The field lost its breath beneath a blue tarp, jugular, veins were piled high. When I release, I like to turn up the TV, I like to keep my distance, I like to forget about you, and when fragmentary I like to *be* fragmentary and not hold steady in an outside version. I like to hear language turn round on itself for its own sake and to imply that the human does not inhabit language. If so, who matters, having narrowly missed a tenure? Is life particularly about reversal of expectations? If you were seven years old, one expectation would remain inexplicable as it hollowed out a lifecourse that included status valences of merenesses. Poetry is saying what you weren't supposed to. A pageant that into history lifts corporate wardrobe decisions. Notes exist for hidden orgasms. Connections make sense when they actually happen. Problem is the silly beaches, the endless coating whose crimpings harden on the sidewalk, and golf. I am safe away again at a remove from questions, and playing my part is someone of high caliber. Charles Wright. Stop saying my name. If dessert is interrupted by a body being dragged, then press the button, or take the order. The veritable sin is critique, particularly objective critique. You see, this day will come around again, and I want to be there.————Any seed that might appear now is now but it could go back in the ground where it began, or where by a finger placed, or where it began before covered by soil blown by the wind. And wind that blows soil over seeds has little to do with now, particularly since the seed is back, moment to moment, passing in our company, as if it saw this, as if we built these things. Wind has little to do with it and it was as comfortable here now that it broke free from itself out of sheer forgiveness for what we did to it, its slow burial, which now has reminded us of something. Now is a good time to acknowledge that every speech, or curvature or barely discernable nick is as relevant as and mirrors constellations as they are announced up there, above an emergent seed. And its skin. And one thing we all know is that our emergent seed is mostly a critique, and to be critiqued is to fail and succeed in the same breath. If I notice a thing out of place above the ground, if any implications are felt, then this so benefits whatever might happen to me that I lash away at the outside world. Below now, below here, the underworld yearning upward, ignorant and uncritiqued. Now bliss above, and bliss below, something will hold us up. A radical film between these things of a film over my eyes yet also between me and what I see, my hand a night, the panoramic of earth's surface. To push the seed back down as the world spews me forth, into itself. Care looks like its opposite. Or is it recognizable? Finally then exposure works, roots emerging like always. They meet, clean out, but can spread laterally. A body reaches upward too. It thinks of a zion train. It builds a gentle villa. Music is heard, as if played by the wind.————And as sure as he was. As arcane as the boots of the legions of worshippers growing up through accumulation of signifiers, I mean of experiences. A light was shed first on what we were then on the reversed though spherical planets. If you consider what might have happened then the question of who fought, or what appears in Asian jungles centuries ahead of their time. If I could understand that question I would be better than I am now. I would not be altered. Frankly, there would be none left. Besides, the real subject was . . . intolerance. And the next most real . . . belligerence. Then came bologna. Then, at rest in the decaying caves, flocks of pigeons breathing the same nameless air we were. Society seemed to give a little. You were quite free in your agency. Then for no reason a pall descended and there were no more forms. Since poetry cannot be understood in its contextual reference fewer and fewer of us write about the world. The tendency is toward artificial order that hides nothing, absolutely nothing, which is a reflection of whatever it was. Points to make: (a) do

you think I should walk near the tiny creak?;
(b) what's the first thing you see when you
walk into the grocery store?; (c) are any parts
of my body frozen?; (d) have I been worthy?;
(e) do I need a cornerstone or do I constitute
one?; (f) how many different things are finger-
licking good?; (g) did you just smile?; (h) is
there anything organic about the monetary
devices?; (i) was it true, what they said?;
(j) how long can you remain safely ignorant?;
(k) if you didn't know something, can you turn
back anyway?; (l) frankly, the gentleness
of the example could not have been more dis-
turbing; (m) molds crack; (n) we're particles;
(o–z) who gaveth instruction to stop think-
ing?————Hide as it would have hidden, or
been constituted by its own boundaries, the
container went through the factory, taking up
space on the surface of earth. If letters are
mailed back and forth, then hide. Or hide in
the luminous significance that was part of the
multiple choice, that was a split second hideous
but ultimately fluid in its open bodily speech of
mouth. A voyeur sees the mouth. As a small
animal, only food, or hunger, certain. Nothing
like speech. So only feeling certain. And feel-
ing a pure song, highways built in its honor.
Did you not breathe exhaust at first, absorb it
through your mother? There is no way to
know the content of a form before making the

form content. One chooses form like a partner, or the next possibly containing body to touch, emerging from traditional barriers. Then it is subject to "have" that is not first hidden and only later broaches far into the poem. I'm not sure what you wanted poems to do. Not sure what you wanted to think. Was it natural, did the other narrative pan out, like Kerouac's, like Pound's? Then, you know, the sign I see every day, for Varrick St., could become historic. The dross, flotsam, refine of sound and sense the paper of mind, glue still wet, rollers not quite evenly applied, my living an attempt to think of doing, enable to drown these surfaces, get my hands in. I can get my hands into almost anything else. Shambles, forgotten. And therefore hide, and therefore experiment. To come this way, describing what I am doing. Imposter. What will you tell my children? How will they know it is you? How much meaning is in this time, in the earth barriers? It must be a universal habit.————I heard someone ask "What happened to poetry?" There were so many syllables in the mouth that it must have been knowledge. Nine-tenths of the time I was frozen, in the bow of an old paniche. The water was there. And now it's language, the thing resisting penetration, like the voice in English, the voice embarked on, unaware that by then to speak of what happened to poetry was like saying "did you hear about World War II?" But I was frightened about not knowing a thing, about pointless being pointless and commenting, so rushing to graduate school. As one attempts to talk or turns ever more decisively toward a warm bed, digested within a boat of ice. I'd never heard such conversation, only heard of Voltaire's statue, near the Pont des Arts. And so, where I was. Suddenly, I went among the people. Suddenly that was a dream. If dark itself spoke, then there was no use timing the interaction, which was between me and the outside forces. Voice on air. Voice whose hand was in someone else's, a man on the quay to which my boat was tied. And within the bow's curved wood, myself. A solar symbolic weakness destined to give birth. Barring what happened to poetry I know I must, at first light, scrape the ice from the walls around my head. And if I thought of Rilke, he would know, if I tore a film from my eye, I could describe it. I could travel south through Spain, proud to write anything at all. But the same hands here as on the boat, the same hands looking nowhere into the future. So back to me now and ten years on, again. They'll finally make sense of things.————How far to swim would not be indicative. On the theory that the poetic pours from any given moment so that no matter what is written there is interest, more likely than not quite strong. There in the excrescence from journal world or human response. . . . What avenues of resistance are still open? Few things seem more ridiculous now than the resistance itself. So that's it, you're full of demands, even the fucking construction worker sweeping the streets maintains resistance, looming girth, hard door, wife and kids in the wash machine. There they are tumbling up and down, going about their business. Culturally determined swim. Just know whom you're speaking to. Just come to rest. Don't think beyond that. If an archway asked you to pass under it, who then would know to walk? A thin universe is better than none, what's on offer. That's called decision. And shoot, I don't really like that poem, I just said I did. There was a sale price and we were it. But we kept calling after that, thinking there was more at stake than just us. And so what, people sing. The fraternal order co-opts its own members. If you're in San Francisco, try to make something up. You'll see. One thing to do is cross the ocean. One gift to make is words themselves. Not thought, but on a surface. The self-referential, watershed, delta bottom. How miniscule our partition, county lines, syllables, odes, food groups, businesses, personnel, us/them. Rages water, water rages and none know how to save themselves. Swimming is one more chance to develop. Light through prisms, faithless. Only white matters. Now, we're grouped today about the bottom-most root. If exception was taken they were quiet about it. To run loosely, after no one could speak. Then the poem lifted.————Even devout I was unable to sift through the tangles. So that I was here sifting through myself, devotional. Taking aim across townships, hovering at borders before taking the cities. They should have instructed us: no one has the best potential commandants. One of my brothers, testing my faith, and one more of myself, gravitating to the selfsame identical seat every day without thinking then thinking. Art emerged from my mind and body. At certain stages we are all without help, our understanding patched in from outside courses, from track light fingertips that collect and cap rage like a squirrel putting acorns in a husk. Here's what I would say to that—each floor has a corner office. That's it. No one else is so well able to serve their purposes. Blindly, before sound catches up to them. A multitude of cranes constructing. Same as the holocaust, must be. Their lives beyond that sectional, their true series of philanthropies. So that I am left in front, handed the long black metal, not smoking, my brother near me. Now change, now turn inside, before investigation can continue. Keep surging blindly back and forth. You'll hit something human. Their search ends at a tall blade of dried grass. This must be certain. I am miles away from my family. Personal observation #2,756. Are you like me? You must be, which is my wherefore. Delete PO#2,756. Back to square one. Poems turn back on themselves. Poems obliterate the stages they contain. They know more than what they say. They care so much for the human that they seem not to care at all. What sequence? The flying must end. You've lied if they take you for lying. Knighted by perception, perception continues. Operatic electronic tone. If I am not still cutting these lines from my hair, then what am I doing? My actions do not count, or only as a distraction.————Nothing became much. Don't bend over. Not unless. But wait. Did that significance, or wait a revolution, carrying, underwater? One penetrable loop you are. One unassuageable being capped lucidly in front of me. What turns to us today surely tomorrow will turn in the inverted direction. What happens internally is a collapsible version. It cheers us along our route, tragically. Ever notice how . . . Naaaaa. Neglecting the night shot, all you've ever tried to do. If you didn't contain so much disturbance I would participate and have genuine particles to eat or brush off my lineaments. Oh, don't give one to her, she's the owner of language, she's the highly erroneous other who narrates countless collections. Lessen the fake determinations. Light the hallway before we stumble. Credence is little to us, who prioritize *now* so fervently that words cannot only not catch up but beg off the pretending. The cover is lifted, hallelujah. There is nothing like the light that gives off what I'm saying. Lances through and through. That terrible bastard. Truth is, this could be more disparate than anything. So don't try to figure it out. Be content not to have been literally buggered. If the whole is beached, fuck it. Gropes for lunch, that's it. And human slime. Look, I can't help but translate what enters my head through my eyes. Garbage in . . . the memorial was really hard to take. The lingering rain made it impossible to see, even inside, near the source. A computer could be more disparate, if that's the intent. Or perhaps one day you'll be discovered as that narrator. When the psychological split is healed. It's simply a mode of journalism. If the earth is a womb, then that's all there are, wombs.————If situations thrive, then go. If a moment exists, then have your farce. If sempiternal malfeasance of language inhibition, if they wait for you in their bodies, then what's to have? Corporations stand behind this motivation to move on, lavender highlight, play across the patios. And to take your own tally, to stand against your own feet, to manage a manger in the first degree. Oh, how hot it was. How awful. But we saw the moment at last and decided to brave it. We chose to love them. We never didn't send cards to each other. We lent cherries and cheerios to the botanical landowners, we bargained and farted and bargained and farted. Just because it was easy and we were made to do so. No matter what side of Petersburg you're from. And the hideously lame, whom we've all rescued. Ambergris filters like an aegis past its watchtower, honing its blasts and hymnals before boiled neighborhood partitions. To be back, or upturned, to saunter with only three bodies, our party name. If not the feet, then what, what of us against land? If not the hands then tuned lost authentication, on an easier flying. For that, for lost categories if moments shielding the basin of tabled thought. Undo the series creators, mention their felicities, or have major instruments approved. No family has more fervently instructed the worldspace to "wait until later." They have a budget that is visible context. They announced a dual population, they proceed to split things against it. Day of the journal writers, who wasted no discernment on ripeness or funny failure. They are only to surface against the planned interior, with something that graces fingerspace and open eye.————What a lot to not see, what a world of the unseen. Now this world within me collaborating, forced forward? I "own" these questions, they are me. What other inhibitions, the rack, the body, the operation, the questioner, the light, the wall, the cave itself. Dawns covert as these who raise us are. To exceed time itself is no laughing matter, though laughter shall have its excellence through us. What shape shall we want from the sea, itself itself itself until we lose our resistance? What tournament of linked flames, ardent after so long staring at our written selves? To savor what was blocked in, or what long ago lifted itself through wood and smoke. What sage umbilical funny bone was you when measurements were solved? Does it matter now? Does tapestry in itself reveal a mist? What certified the inner stretch so families could collapse their marks? How did so many of the frivolous gain the proscenium marks of lordship and country fairs? I know, before we let ourselves go again we'll pour out our lingering. *We are not free yet.* And when it comes, the muscles in the head retreat into clarity and insight, where they belong. What did we do when that hill arose, lifting its strange light from glowering brush?————Strange labors, repeated. I must remember the orange color after I die. I was so orange while I lived. And living I became orange, I thought I was dead, I thought I was preparing for later thoughts. And now California is like Florida, and even meeting on the beach we could not exchange things, we could not admit or congratulate any of our efforts, any of our indications that later would follow, beyond the lameness of parenthood. If one remains warm, orange is a factor. If one lets fall a river one has let fall everything. There is a meter, there is a frame of reference, a limit on time. Sabbath is a day of mourning, a day of time within our frame of movement. The element of our regenerative lusts rises to accusations. No matter who might tell us, we wander on in our own hair, a nebula of listing fragments of disinclination and nonfulfillment. A rude yet open line of documents pacing beyond reward. Alone against a charged labor, repeated until the name is changed, lossless functions metastasized like pollen in a season's grip. Who taught the choruses to say "What does it matter?" Who showed them in excelled arrangement the wingspan of a cormorant? Its dark timeline, its nothingness in the sun before its minutes-long submersion? Those who need to say have said and constitute a favor to the dead, when clocks strike or buds give way, something I've always said. To labor in dread, repeatedly, is its own lesson, since a sharp stone above us and a mire beneath command a surface beneath, above.————And if you were to know. What would you know? Would it be you or me? If you sank far below would you suddenly see yourself? Or part of yourself for a moment, then you would see a purple tree? My own paradise is wishing you, but from a remove that might as well be someone else. If the gravel were piled high, if the mounds slipped and shifted until they were flat, then you would experience your own frost, then burial would be just an idea. My ordering sensibility could never listen to you. That was when it defended itself against you, all the while losing you. And if we sang about terrified shade, that was a gesture, and you captured it. No one could relegate the purple tree to your fearsome categories. Suddenly the gathering bustle of the ordinary world is head above the heart's cry for you. Just then no one remembers their grand permission to invoke the chemical burning you labored to forgive. No single technical termination of you, no beam of consequence outlined the possible territories of your granted wishes. Who should say, as if the spherical hymnals were under your control, tabled in your fingertips like glass instructions for gloves. I have to be significant, I linger and hang from you like a tied stone. So severe you must be pursuing the leery, insipid limelight. If you speak to me I'll remove the gathered paperweights and float against the hardness that controls me. If you punctuate the destinations and a biblical turn makes sense, the vast insouciant wisdoms thumbing now and again on tone's life. If you gave that life its gaze, is it time now to turn away? If something lied, how would you respond to it forever in memory, as if you knew it never lasted but knew of nothing else?————If I am writing about that then where is it? It appears but not without each of the elements, much like a fine haircut that succeeds in the necessary and not so necessary reflection of what it was that day. Oh poor you. Oh poor imperfect century. I might have had different caseloads of paradigms to present, but I stuck with the post-war stuff. I'm a troubadour I thought but then his prancing distracted me. What was it that day, whereon were raised mounds of carnality? Sin couldn't be worse than standing near him. Scents went about my nostrils, causing pains even now unguessed. Remember the thing you won't remember, since you were never there? Now to speak of his meditation. It must have been me, but other opportunities were clear to me as well. I'm not sure if his eyes were open or shut. I can't possibly be a redeemer, with so much failure. So much since the shaded circumference of a financial center full of books (we no longer refer to financial "centers"). And the five fast tall men went from foot to foot, resisting the urge to hold on as the train rumbled through the East Bay tube. If only he would leave. Or open his eyes. Then our meanness would expose the other meannesses and let day be as nice as it likes. As told, Holocaust museum honors with a wall essentially words the Moroccan Jews. The French and the departure for France. Don't ask me a single question. Don't lay down the barren light. What more is there of objectivity, where we know what feeling is? It must be something happening to us now, it must be standing next to me, in the person of a tiny man in happy mocha. How is time like that? Even if the urgency of strength has fallen on the serious open eye, we know what feeling is. And now what's left, if there are other wheres to go? The pen was meant to give away, no matter what the chances were.————How could you be on to something? Well today the world happens to have happened with a smattering of normalcy or whatever you like, until mid-week. And what could I have seen at last mention? There was a last bet, wager on spectacle available and out there, discriminated. At least that's the first place, and explains most everything for now. So there's what you want and what I want and a large distinction that's behind us. How did you know the resolution when you saw it? Well, within me there was a poem of place, and a shy awkward spirit entered the world in front of me. The stanzas linked to the upper bookshelves and a slow distinction was an extension of the sunrise. Few others are awake now few others are forgotten. Hope is a kind of tube equivalent to an elevator shaft in a very tall building, with a wizard inside it. So that both of us like two hoboes knew to be billboarded with strange understandings of inchoate desires, with haunted backgrounds the true absorbents of the parkways. How could I know? If something's there beyond these lines of sight it would need to be captured musically, a margin of breath like a walkway around a lake or pond. If being becomes smaller then you are no father any more. Being so small it is only graffiti hidden near an old highway, relics of identity. Which is why you had to come, a relic of your own bliss. There's little chance of learning if a light fails and labor can't investigate. One poetry over another and we must have been resting when the ballroom opened, en fin the invitees going home to their parental beds. A surge of striking timberlines, matter for eager generations I pass the airport every day.————This is what you were entitled to. This Wednesday keeping to yourself. Even then, there was no way to support. Even afield, the censors kept their hands away. With punctured rhythms. Heat blisters commanding the entire surface, beauty just a way to trace the spheric dead skin. What will you tell them? I mean, in general. Or what will you tell them when they come to your door? I'll tell them to read the newspaper, instead of this. Those are the choices and if there's poetry there then why do you need me? The blizzard comes again. I'm sure he'll get herpes. I wouldn't want to be him. So much contact. Not enough mystery. At the level of stone the warders recommend rationing and continue debate. Lights out, so let's think about it. Know you, and you've exceeded the limit arches have been drawn to. No one could resist ladling the heavy soup that day and no one could speak quite like. She did. I was a silent partner, all the while he was able to keep looking over my shoulder. I was silent in my hands and in my expectations that growth was sure to continue, or that this must be the moment. The time has come to watch someone pick their nose in front of a computer screen. There are not enough tissues in the world. Finally the curtain came down on you walking across the street, or on you sitting around. How's that for a green integer? My copy of the *Ethics* is in the top drawer with the socks and underwear. Pajamas beneath that. Technically, this is my fortress, so relax. This serum is like a catapult. Fight for it. Then at your leisure you'll see us waiting at the window with all of our highest criticisms. Swim with me, oh swim with me once. Swim as if no one watched, as if we had all we needed.————This, as opposed to an old motion in place. The bright orange that came forward to meet you. Then the daily events. Did you notice those? Did you come to believe me, that I said what I'd been thinking for so long? Did you look at me closely? The simple question is an abbreviated veil starting with an empty tooth. Now that's not the right way to shame and you've clearly entered the wrong restaurant. I have no defined rhythm with which to morph. Impossible to identify. If you would pick it up, only that. I'd feel better about getting closer. The shower you took has pretty much been replaced by a new congeries of fumes. Looks like another hygienic delay. And what drives me, what parcels of land, what investigative dilemma in terms of nearby age-comparable emphasized neighbors? (Don't forget: you are your own logic.) Instantly the this and the that. Time forever, and that's just the way they feel. Certain prepackaged ideas are rubbing against me and I'll need to run off right now to the dim candlelight, epic turkey fumes, sculpted table legs, bins full of broken tablets. Oh well, nothing can be said to be full. When did we know this was happening? (The stupidest question in the world.) Or, in the meantime, lakes, gargantuan, bridle groves, incomparable shade, a troubled play of surfaces. Again? Approaching from behind, "this" cables forward to my inner self and I turn without turning, create wide lines just like the swirl in the ice cream. Notably today is cloistered off from its suggested clouds and firmaments warn the interlocutors. If this was doubt, then they would remain there. If this was distance, then why were the birds given it as well? Over there, it's your bypassed self, any of the links crisped into hand are brittle entreaties.————The definition of an imaginative worldview. And still I'm not sure where I've been, or where I am (except near a post in the woods marking a trail we've missed, so long ago). That was a way to see more than a few things at once, a transcendence of the eyes that no mechanical eye could yet relieve. And worse things than living. I'm sure there are. Whatever is not yet works as signature. He takes the wheel of whatever ship, his own mind, a here houseful of loose molecules, an undefined bend in the road, the sagacious capture of body parts and latches into the trembling abatements of sugar and spice. One fury is not enough, I need three, or even a dictionary definition under discussion before we left the station and you became whatever world you were. She was our most honored guest, and she escaped. This was what we couldn't have fathomed but slipped into anyway, to merely spend the rest of our lives there. I'm a captured professor. Are you? If your teeth fail do not mitigate your desires or derogate on view. Wishbone. If the ceiling is too low come back to the filter or replace the original substance, the beautiful chemical substrate trudging through a zero-balanced memoir, behaving like an ocean-abutting cliff. Who said "belief" is the same one who marveled at the words "Palermo" and "piston," which before long were not words but apologies, wrong decisions punished by the wrong decisions. The bog who was crying was not pitied. *There's no paradise, there is only your mind.* War is unserious in that it is a product of someone's imagination. The recovery of sight by the blind, a mode of description that has never been tried. Who imported the windows? Who did the work? We ourselves *are* the several networks, which will never be captured again. They reach back into their own salvation, succumbing to nothing.————Instant opening on round declension. Man riding a horse pulls up in front of our house. If the earthquake were to hit now we would be devastated, even assuming we were all fine. A cloak keeps saying that it bleats out truisms. Why worry? Knowledge comes, angles of truth arrive, the body reveals its inclinations, almost instantly.

We know exactly what to say. The general fold of the field corresponds to the brow. At each historic intersection the field reappears. It becomes a legitimate biography, it borrows its interest from the media, as plain as can be. It continually suggests itself for the starring role. It tries to look at its own thinking. But still, through the opening in the sky, it descends like a UFO. The whole world is changed by these visitors. They subject themselves to all of the earthly charms, the attendant griefs. Finally they die, never to be seen or heard from again. It was only because of our own death. That was why this happened. The war was a result of an adolescent fear, frustration with the sheer mystery. Therein our foundation that we were not given to know. I am aware of all of the new construction. It interlineally blocks my way. I show up holding truth and significance, I show up with a surface and sugared map. Does this turn the day, the tide, the tension. Brazen lingerers and coupled analysts point at what it was. A facade that's built is still a facade and still built. Awakeness that hears, a head that fumbles, a watermark that seeds the truth. If none of these are openings. If favors are withheld. My life was spent in purchasing. Now I have a new life. No more wind. Just the opening. Even against our roofs still the birds arrive. Solidify a future. Just the opening. Whistle, contingents dive in. What happened over there, the report of so much sound? The news shows birds diving in water.————Orange in its flight away from me becomes entirely different, deliverance, a distance baked into endlessness. No one here was doing what I was, even from a distance. Anyway how could it be known who I was, any of a thousand soft shields, any market rising and falling, the third season of what we thought we were doing. Perhaps I'll die at the moment of a shift in color, when nothing happens except a constant visual sloping one word to the next. Even so color inaugurates its own abilities, it matches the seed blowing on the air. It carefully tells a story we've never heard before, it changes like a powerless sun. Decayed by light we should know how to shift ground, then caution against collaboration and seeking frameworks. If whole, then save it for later. Back at the home base of color, of seasons really, when something dominates. I can easily tell you how it was. I can secure vast areas of crime, where animals walk ahead. Who are they? you ask. None of us knows. Probably they have the same fixations in the buried gestational matrix as the seasonal delimiters, as fog itself. And time tables, ways to talk, warnings and party lights shifting away. Without the weed of consolation then espiritu is warbled over Sky Intercom 7. That's something, but still the fragmented tiger and then a grammatical taint to the winter cup. Gifts attend any child, mysteries attend any fright, any lush cornerstone approaching. How do you see me? As someone with pageants and toenails and liver enough for two? What's the label for what just happened? Not knowing its fun to break or drive ahead. It's fun to pulverize toilet rings too, going together.————You tend to decline the topics. You tend to sit and stare until no more is left. You tend on one hand to look at the portrait and be forgiving but on the other hand to give in. A lesson, if anything, taken from one city to the next. The people here will appreciate what they've seen, the spirit of the millennium. I'm certain of the fog now, I know it's created by the mist off the waves. I know if it hits something large enough it stops. I circulate the broad aspects of peering up into the light, which is when the carts full of goods emerge. The tangled sadnesses, I guess they've done. Then with the same awesome momentum, the sea returns. It submerges many of the poems of the island nation. It submerges the offices of the publication of the poems. It lingers in thought when confronted by ministers of exchange. What would they say? That time is removed from the exchange, that miniscule labors are everywhere? Sit back, relax, enjoy the ride. Words have implications. Words as corpses are thrown around like garbage. I know, but I'm not saying. I'm not sure I can get a handle on the true conception. It recedes in front of me. Again, you reject my conception. Again the awful thinking of a pure evening. We have little more than the cylinders we bump into in the dark. I'm sure I could shave a few days off the schedule. I think it's worth encapsulating the foreign matter. I'm sure in the senate chamber there's a storm brewing. What a way to behave. Constant horizons appearing the only sense there is. I was exhausted by what you were saying. I was then emboldened by the possibilities of content. How ordinary are these extremes? That's the day of the goodbye, since everyone has one.

I wouldn't know what you were doing. I wouldn't be able to take those tests, to take those tests with rue. Then it would start all over. These were different *walls*. These were white moving inward, windowed, chimnied, folding, vertical. We communicated across the folds, every test pointing to now. On board ship, they collaborated. They shared what had come up the night before. The circumstantial lamplight. Take out your wallet. Take out a 10 x 3. Then, as if you were complete in the allotted space, the partial room with those other people hiding somewhere (isn't every word

precise?), the offerings wilted like conse-
quences of the past. The world hits with a face
blowing its rhyme, soil against a blue sea. If
what you've seen is like what we already have,
then keep doing it, no matter what the water
looks like. If what you said is like a bullet pierc-
ing through, then we'll dig until our eyes glint.
A metal sheen is thrown around my upper
home, the things that have to happen now.
Like seasonal green that drowns a living tree.
Like elephants pressed against a retaining wall,
their notions are but three. I'm sorry about the
poorest shards, which at night barely number
three. They don't escape us, or remark us, un-
less we test them and we see, on the north side
snowing. On the south side melting, I'm not
sure we included thee. Strings to earth. Con-
stant description attaching. In a box. Nothing
to do. Until we notice an amount from "out
there," which becomes a story, of later days, on
the front porch, no longer in a hurry, not car-
ing whether the world sang or succumbed.
Our formal attire, this pustule or your own
body. Give thanks. This rest of the body, for
safety. Let's sing about it—the rest of the body,
the rest of the body. If I were counting these
within variant degrees of space there would be
different measures, depending on the primeval,
depending on a sheet of something firm, that
finally became spiral, and therefore that un-

varying song, which is simply a way to shift outward, the face of disease. Now, here's what's contained in nothing: bright neighborhood, no one very long said to be lain low. And if I were. Asking you, that is. Asking you by the fact of what I am. Still he has nothing to do. Still my interlocutor reaches out. What does a feeling person make? The sun will be a soul again, one soul. The sun will have its components justified, it will have land in the same fractions as labor. Happy then, like a wassail or a shimmer. Looking then, over the countless nothing doorways. Having forgotten touch, labor returns. It downplays and belittles its ostensible pattern. It says, not this way comes anything. How old do you have to be? Since I have been asking that question, the spoiled spot has grown. You would not be able to fathom a mountain, you would run into trouble from day one. You would freeze, even against the face of your father, of her father, running naked (until this year). Seasons have shed your life for you, the very service we've come to rely on. Interesting maturations happened in those decades, but now it's up to us, to look squarely into the whirlpool, naturally occurring. Ah the banging! Why wouldn't it make sense at any other time? Only in New York. Only with multitiered arpeggios wrapped snuggly around its iron head. When we are old, charity is outside of us, tension is disturbed. In Hollywood, the composers have their own lounge, where they sit shouldered by a crowd, despairing of their wives. If right comes from such capable hands, it must be a great craft to extinguish it. The rating's gone. The nude escapes. Pool parties where generations get enflamed. When it's my time I hope my Eggos will flash upward, I hope my fish holes will be stockinged with fashioned constraint. It was impossible to know the full count of ballets or mistakes. Don't give me money, it will only drag me down. Here, let me impart what my mother imparted to me. Make sense of things. Make the golden shaft rushing overland toward your soft center into the payoff, not the paydown. Like a symphony we gather every year, chanting. What light would you make, if there was light? What face would be in front of you if you had any face at all? I forget who the patron was, surely a member of the tribe, surely a dancer nearby. I forget what shapes were left unsaid, but at night we weren't supposed to speak shapes anyway. To break from those requirements. Even if you could stay with one poem invisibly counting a continuous song, just right against an oracular opening, oval lung. I wrap my shoes around a safe reply, I am nowhere to be found. I have fled the relationship. I am nowhere in this round hall, or this restaurant/bar. I have a wardrobe. There are mixed results, there are mixed greens, jack cheese, what's around me. Music creeping from our pores, each layer infiltrated, one atop another, for such tithe as self is made of. My whole eye is a tread the earth makes, my "Hey wait, now we're being told." Now we're locked in an embrace. 3-year facial. Why so much awesome sadness? If you don't have a vision, there are ways around that. If you're in a cubicle we can help you. We can get you to where you won't need a great body of unified ways of looking. It was the moment when a neutral body arose. Translating nothing was disgusting. Everyone was the same height. Each labored jonquil was a Gerry curl. Each sequence looked the same but only today, with its porches and platforms of the tongue. To adjust to the new wave, were the tiny bodies too old for that? Were they fortunate to "succeed"? What else would happen before the whole disconnected communicative apparatus shrunk to a pea? That frozen afternoon voices connected across questionnaires, backward comprehension of birth tension. Make no remark about my intelligence. As if it were a poem. As if it knew what to say or what it was about. My heat arises from other sources, other sources talked about. The long conversation with my father. The delectation of waking up one morning, perhaps alone, perhaps against a wall. Intelligence, place before a feeling came. Emboldened to watch the body breamed. Nothing grows around the body except this. We have special gloves, we hear special notes. We cable to the spheres what won't fit in a message we could cable. If only to repeat it. Three women walk contemplatively along an empty road, near a warehouse, early morning. They thought of no poem. I moved along, I believed something else entirely. Since what I am: heat, urgency. Far away. What did they think? Would the world be going to hell? What forest would you yourself provide? How many angels looked for you across the room? The orgasm is a way to recover from the walking we have done. I serenade like the jostle of machinery, I resemble the heavenly matrix, which is etched across a dome. In the place outside of here the violent animals roam. Is that where we should go? First voices, gravelly, experienced, must be heard. First the world's intelligence takes hold and there's no question of my interference. First a wave of being every day. First to know what you know, to know what you do not know. How was it that clean, when you were thrown out of your house? Who else was in the room with you—nothing genuine, legs, feet in place to withstand a precise attacking? We'll always grieve our round numbers together, think of it, think of what time allows. Particles

even now settling sideways into the hush. I
don't know what continuation is. At 40, we
start to wish for not only more ice cream but
for the kids to eat it with. By that time we'll
have been out of touch for twenty years. The
neighbors are heard wandering near each other,
in the nick of time. The gendarmes have soul—
something to turn to and the lions feed on
Wednesday nights. Thin devotion, for the rest
of the week, thinking the hunt, what visitors
mostly observe. With the right chemicals, nu-
trients, that is, we leave off sparing these *new*
souls. Like marbles they slavishly follow cost-
effective inclines. They *result*, which allows
them to be monitored. Then when finally
books are published about the timing metrics,
we holler from the kitchen porch. Constitu-
tions—look, let's just say that our tears incul-
cate their own magnitudes. And if you laced a
canyon with a freight train, why didn't you
peek at the final descending acknowledgments,
the white centered text scrolling slowly but
surely? Lowly but purely. Hmm. Static seems
to forbid us to leave. If not for the announce-
ments there would be no knowing (a) when
the tickets were checked, or (b) the valence of
the oppressive technologies. Now, back to *Liv-
ing*. Back to what part of your body you heard
lies in. The green knight. Something appeared
when I was not there. Some shy official put up

boards everywhere. And to know an expense report is to be one. Look, what we really wanted, to indicate the washboard syndrome. I personally trace the troop movements back to the invention of gloss. None of the other nasty habits could stand that kind of test, shaking at the root. The period of waiting seems to interrupt the functioning but holds sand and syllable of its proper cause. Two sides of a river have divorced each other and there's no telling what the new plans are. Each of the faces turns inland. When it's time for the last breath, we survey the last round then peer through that. I don't care what kind of shelter is current, just that certain derogations take place. The whole neighborhood was impacted, but in a good way. Not necessarily by our policies, though it's possible to look to the studies that were done and talk some more. Nowadays no one is left, from back then, and we're concerned with present disturbances. We mostly accost them with our daily thing but it's nice to put a nice face on it later, right before bed. Still couched in the appeasement, this is when our real love of the agreement comes into play. Its terms function as organs, the word for heart, the word for head, the word for when and where. Deeply grateful we notice in the morning that the entry is clean. The mud falls from the clean faces of the officials who imagined this for us.

Not until much later in the day does the abstraction of junk become a blue factor. By the time of the nuptial we're torn by the old linkages. Lust like blushed potatoes stuck to a skillet, smell of old oil, taste hidden behind mouthwash. There are a few more dreams than I would have said. I'll leave off counting and calculation. Ropes are manufactured instantly and everything between our hands looks like the middle of a plot assigned by a disappearing office. Ordinary gentlemen must have been watching. They placed bets in this windlessness and general fixation. Then operatives operate on operation, nonstop resurrection, a perfectly erect election, an indication that grimly led to the end. Each prelate was a particle of reality, any given pope succeeding in office. None of the popes lacked calm, prelates and constables crowding around. But it's more than I could meander into this morning, these general affinities. Let's not climb too far together, I mean alone, once we've separated and the cable cars are whisking away party members. Too many functions of my value look like reservoirs spreading fever. And that flock compensates, anytime really, for the lost flock of last week. If it's not too much, tell me what you're thinking. The bullet stops because we turn to the mundane fixes. We turn to the shapelessness of custard. Sex tags our libido for who we are. Any excuse will do. A haggard shape, every word lopsided. Different things have been bought for me. Released from thinking, each history is a little horny. I've never been with you, either. I never caught sight of what you were thinking. We've agreed to believe. What if she never told the truth? How many cycles do we go through? Does anyone have the time? My organic metaphor, my shoe size. I have passed into the solidity of my own head. Now that you've met yourself, say you're sorry, say what might happen. The hammers and saws are the noises of morning, as if definitions above the sky were like orbiting flowers. This constitution, that constitution. I'm not sure who is looking. I'm under the traffic in a tunnel of crimes. Any tube would have done but our sudden riches purchased transitional comforts, like syrup and honey. To believe that she's there because the markers are, because in holly bush and frock the instruments rust. If seeds on air then feet on metal heart-ground. Eyes on paranormal ordinary melt. I could be any one of these machine-made objects, since I built the machines. If paperwork then roll up your sleeves. Content yourself, divagate, but coffee your spittle and wash your eye. Building maintenance, candy sales, bus routes. Philosophy is crazy. Her parents were dead but they left her the Mercedes. The new models were already shipping. I guess entanglements don't pay off, but put the ringing phone in your pocket. I would shake until the cows arrived. I would be a harbor caught within a margin never trying to touch you. In multitudes of exits the savage lines appeared, and as we were leaving I wanted to "show up." In multitudes of texts different natures crawled, with none of us to trace them. They shook as they faded. Then suddenly the voice of intimacy. He held the door for us and said it was time to go. We had our doubts. Then present company consisted purely of the well-adjusted. Suppose these voices were not following a pathway, that they had been stretched across the temporary partitions. And who was to question this caliber of instruction, if it could mount such a resurgence in the aspect confronting it? None of the men have lipstick. How unpleasant they've become, their combativeness, their sexual racing forward. That presence, someone simply sitting there, retracing habits and collecting leaves. Have you in your stupid cape been able to be yourself in front of yourself? What is supposed to feed the cohesion? At your own expense, with all your might, you uttered "might." But what awful gradations have you now found enpalmed. If everything is grey and dandelions are hiding. That means it's time to reconsume the favor. And what to do, as expressions & wounds are licked, as counterpoise is analyzed and fragrance is abolished like the luster on the docks, for removal all over again? The fantasy is a questioning fantasy, of being able to question. Then recursive personal imagination before the bell rings and the door closes. Harmony is nothing if not hard, music the world makes. The nasty looks, reduplicated staring, clean but for the dust of exhaust. I was clean, too, I want to say. Instead I throw a rock, go home, look up. Instead, as things happen, a paroxysm derives its outline against a burning from within, from without. If we show each other to each other's communities. Toil loops its ladders past the mundane avenues. It's never funny. Had he meant something to her, had he fallen in the ruin, had the blast meant the false-ness of dimness of a pageant of ruin? Shapes of self pity renumber in the stockyard. Existence has little pulp, but appears to shadow what be-comes of native folk. Please remember, if a small name replaces you then it comes forward pronouncing its own wish. There's one thing my mind adores. It is the typical compliments. It's what we'll put our money toward. A be-lieving bubble. A tragic spate of concurrent trouble. Then what happens, the altarpiece, the ray that woke somehow. Even if I were to hurt myself. This is only a drawing, with cap, nose, mouth, on a structure that prevents the intru-

sion of hard objects. You didn't. I mean you
yourself said it. You yourself did it then said
then woke up early and went out, to a place. I
was anxious, but my teeth knew what to do,
parachutes were cheap in those days, dogs were
awful, handbooks got us started, state fair let-
down, whatever else on the list that was named
at the meeting. In the field the lions cry. They
carried lanterns, they offered madrigals when
our eyes longed for salt. I'm sorry but that
chain, between us or any other oddity, is gone.
In fact, there's less to do than you think. The
polarities and pachyderms having really the
same skin tone as what of ourselves we see, re-
sult in concupiscent shelves & airways. And the
luster's where I want to be and am, if you have
followed. In fact it's nearly nighttime but I'm
sure I'll choose to stay. Grandstand your con-
gratulations, ration food and blood. Ration the
r's, the a's, the tides. This morning in any case
the beaches are gone. The gloss in our galoshes
shines with fire. The nit's solved and you're
welcome to leave. We have to stride, in
thought, to a birdhouse or beachhead. Once
achieved, the shade of our still hinging topic
steps into an untimely repetition. Once re-
trieved, we struggle to look at the top results. It
will catch us, I'm sure it will, though not be-
fore I finish writing. There are two entities to
keep watch over, a shield and a sword. They

suggest completely foreign stories but nonetheless the same one, the lackluster, polluting, overdone one. There is no thought only being with a character called thought or only being, irretrievable friendship. If you were anyone you were someone who saw these elements. Orders of grocery store magnitude I'm not sure you understand. It's simply in the way I was standing there, not a commodity precisely. I've left my trash on the train. I've pitched in. I've for God's sake groomed and please acknowledge me. No more of these roads will be built, no more reductions are going to manifest. Standing, in utter terror. Running wild like a woman standing. How many men have offered their shaken retentions to the coordinates and sand strips and sticky things? The poet-mother was the white light pretending, any fortieth capsule of the day. The poetic insouciance was what mattered and matured before the rainwash was catalogued or reserved. If that was the subject of ordinary lights then worthy increments were true, even rescued ones. No more blithe returning, relying on the market for a good time. In line of lumber languages are going to live, you must love, love on until landscape. I'm certain to have so many tickets, so many stratagems simultaneously in play. Could you have a "say" bank, as defunct as graying cows, which we've read about, their treatment and poor health. Got to go. That's certainly a nice organization. Wheat, measured in percentage bone, is hard held. It leaks onto the pretty lawn. Cable crews fix a network. It's nice though. I come back to it. Nothing can possibly be better than the daily journey, children shipped overseas in containers. No fantasy more appropriate than human cargo, preholocaust relocation. Hey let's ban subtlety, let's nose our way into the back alleys, Arby's and the nauseated retrofit of what went wrong. If one thing was going to, I mean if one of the armies looked good, or if one of the catalogs came in the mail, something to do with Stravinsky, or if records were overflowing, or if combinations failed, I would still participate and precipitate what was juncture contact. Stress, mingle, believe. And by that I mean I was standing alone at shores adjacent to lineations, dreamt annual music that once existed like green light. Removal is so stunningly satisfying that only its incessant occurrence creates epic boredom. But consider, contemplate as if nothing has happened since bread was born in your own hands. Graves swerve, filled with Gravensteins. We stood until doing nothing was the most effective display. If you're going to dig, I suggest here near me. Come and sit and *listen* to me. Poetry nothing but nothing more than a way of going, fully clothed. If we are not exposed then I suggest forgiving. I am not wont to think about my salt. And to sidle, sable thinking about revealing. If Plato is not well I can't imagine the ordinary. It is not well, it is not well. Just now the "if" came true. Bay Bridge of philosophy, of interchangeability, sanctity, the one, the same. Nothing about it, most of all its soft voice, remains. With so much appearing, what are we left with? Interwoven angioplasty, Starbucks, $30. Jane, always June, no matter how much we throw at her. Bulbous with belief, we space the sheets and wait for answers. Smaller the latecomers fill their quicksilver links, their summaries. I'll be visited by the shades again. No one will believe it, but it's true. Strange surge as if related. Going down the mountain, going up the mountain, then we come back. The shame was the overwhelming acceptance that twice forged ahead without us. That twice in its impressions of metal wound up far away. More of me has released the sculpted metal of our names, like it was the outside world. Our cleanliness disturbed, we began thinking of changing what we were doing. We began to be and then returned to being, after we ate. The generation blinked on and off, and then the rest of the world. The slow man has disturbed me once again. When will he make up his mind. Romantic structures, or syntax, are perhaps singular in that they are worthy of our devotion. They undergird fancy and what comes back to us. The marquee is replaced by permanent neon saying one thing alone. The image may have come from a golden penitentiary. We should use it one day soon and make breakfast for those we have a fondness for. Strange knowledge comes. Unusual brides peering up the isle, purchasers in line but not seriously, not crying. If they had built this place not here but over there, the generations would have moved around it, the single most prevalent image would have come sooner. At that adjustable date, I take my way. I eagle forth to Oregon and wander back to town. I speak my lonely paradigm and look like rain that's come and gone. How do you create the bridge yourself, how does your body fit into a mold, helping DNA succeed? If fluorescence is long then what about the bushes clumped together in the meadow? If you'll hold me responsible then the conclusion will replicate its haunting nature outwardly. Even ontologically I refuse the purpose, I consist in a persistence beyond the money of the man. And a neighbor reappears, swirling in unbalanced pride, portraying what they have to inculcate. Place hands on either side of the box, the cause is worth more than a single hostage. The cause like a book follows me into new realities, my native Spain, my ability to look new. What did they reveal when orange was you and then you became a highlight? Basic equations were lived with singularity, and change meant more to the solace of pretenders than milky ways. And to be right to be ontologically right and more than right. Now here is a man who is heedless even of his own words. Is that so? Is the authentication complete in the sense that almightys resist? If the generality is so close why can't they just walk over here? There is a danger in collection, I mean collusion and when we come together we are real but still sleeping. To wander through whatever hills, to linger in a giant face covered in conclusions, pained by any introduction. Is it to gamble to love this way, is it justified to stay at home when builders are on the roof? You paid them; I helped you live. Against a peak, a rabidity, motionless, declaiming—what will I do now, if not proceed, my steps exactly your steps? My fights more and more like battering what was there but *now* lives another universe. Surely you've heard of what collects, stripes are how we look at the living now. To survive with someone looking at you, coming down to a place that feels like what we see outside. Soon we'll be there, looking for a way to get back in. Orpheus? Does it happen? There's some sort of glow there. Certainly there's some kind of glow. We feel it there. Arms out. Chest high. Head raised. Ball of feet firm and hard, up high. To be as high up. To have been shown how to feel. There was nothing wrong with it. Shoved back and forth. Elevated ideas. The one thing I enjoy about working in a crowd is that by watching me they keep me awake, on my toes, firm in my delight. Ah, I say to the night. Where with no features random fathers look about for talk. Despair, oh impossible. My curling about you is like a wound over fresh sutures. Time was it was said to me. Behaving like canyons to each other. It must be solace. It must be what I said, not what the critics said to me. Our articles themselves have faith. In its forms near and far, faith is broken. A high arch appears when the flagpole bends over the tunnel. That's where all our interpretations were. I'm not reading what you thought I should, only Gemini, only fearful names. They were all implanted on the open gaze. Surging into the higher domain. Orpheus had nothing left to do. He would never say what there was or how we should behave. Why be afraid if there was nothing poets understood, nothing they could fear? Fragments of what came in, filaments of a view. That's what the temper looked like, that was it when the act came into view. Calculated time of seeing each other, calculated interview. But it went on all night, her breasts a pillow like the sharp knowledge of a coffin. What else is there to live down, to fill the already filled fields with, the frameless infrastructure and talking. Tread heavy mystery. Do not fight mystery. You and me. Declaration, as if appearances would change and you knew what was going to happen. To structure ourselves silly. And how so sillily structured, pursuing knives in air? My ohms are the lines of fate, wishing they could come to me sooner. To be a brother, looking, peering beneath a heavy plod, approaching it like shells in waves. Knowing is one moment in however many, but once there we're damned. I forget, was it no shoes on your feet or no feet on the seats? And one thing about the body is wherever it goes the filaments follow after, magnetized. Even if magnetism has yet to be explained, we can still use it, bucking the system by other means, in our memoirs, in our mansions wrapped securely about our inner cores, fires warming us beyond this outside world. The blisters of watching so many beheadings, ouch. No more mumbling is necessary, but what's on deck? The great sin could have been the warehouses, just a bunch of tin really with nothing inside, or in plying a satanic sack. Largeness is beauty, but without the visible intent of it we are discussing lawn care. The decision is backward to what links we'd like to draw to anything there. If the decision is calculated in front of your face then maybe you'll trust me. If Socrates were still alive then I'm not sure I'd be saying this. Anyway, how much space is there for us to remember what it was like yesterday, when everything pointed toward tomorrow and nothing was itself except our sons and daughters. If I return to anything it will be to the sin of paternity, which brought me face to face with a confusing document. Some kind of monkey, mirrored, uncaring. What I've done is march straight to my room, plotting, spinning out. How did I arrive at a wish to come here? Just a little last night, when the awful drugs came up. And even genuine generation and its accumulation en fin, or shall I withhold every single bizarre story, as linguistic moments, as tirades that circle the top floors, for days. Lately while walking down the street I've been contemplating the reality of the feminine. A rather stupid question, since how would I know, but it seems to have an effect on me. I'm pretty sure razors are the opposite of air, that poets aren't allowed to show off, and that age when it beckons you seems like the right thing to do. At least the colleges say so. At least when we agreed on sly performance there were nurturers in the room. Nocturnally, nothing is shared, the awful shavings complete the atmospheric partition, weather shifts on the way to Europe. Without

being shy of, say, building a boat the reinforce-
ments get scattered in tapestries, the bulge is
the binge is the barge, fine dining finding din-
ers lying finally forgotten. It resists with spades
of cash meandering in imagination, a true birth
in destination. The awful signatures come back
like visibility strictures, the theory of air was
proffered by a dirty man. To sign away a liveli-
hood is just like sitting near a broken curb.
Sometimes you look over and stick a world-
view to it. Think about those constructions
and the multitudes shaking like no one else
who's sick and half in the other side. As I gen-
erate I turn, an I, and I wane but still adore/ab-
hor a buildup. My performance is not at all my
position, the magi come no matter what. With-
out looking negative there's no way to behave.
The shock of it was its sword, the shame of it
was gone over slowly. There were no little
words about it. It was something I had no way
of knowing. Not whether I was more or less,
not whether contemplating something defi-
cient, the order of the world changing to be in
line with it. Each axiom had its kernel to be
aligned with, as if I were a kernel myself, can-
tilevered, nearing the place at which the turn-
offs dwindled, since they had escaped the plan-
ners' minds, they had been allowed to lock
themselves away, into overgrowth, untrav-
elledness, a constitution ranged about us, the

staring individuals, not remembering. The snow was lost and lonely, like the brain not able to imagine itself, just a collection of sections hard to contemplate for its animality. At one level I decided that there was a patch on my head, keeping my behaviors in, and the patch was something I could feel. And I did search for it, and it came to me like none of the other days. Like gold valves I carried with me, as if my legs could move or even ordinarily the factors leading to present understanding could (but aren't) held in the hand but were just team styles anyway. Otherwise it would just be me. In that fourth category of wind outside prediction I had no doubt we'd be found. At starting points turning round, a naturalist was lurking. Any portentous congeries of mourners was our limping dream held in hand, masticated, let exist since he was not tied to what he was, strange and interesting exactly because he let things exist, and he was none and knew he was because he let things be as they were. To be this interesting! How interesting was Columbus to be around? The snug lists, as if the cabbage freely grew. The first formations. This torrential world. This world in which I hear the words, in which I came first and last to see the components of what I belonged in and first and last to shed alternation toward evening, which is not now. Ruthless deductions, one felt

that she should move then it was true then it
happened again and again, ruthlessly. Our
arms shy of what they might have been doing
now to keep the rest of us intact. The sensation
is of genesis, of an old intelligence burgeoning
but no longer having a place in the world. He
was a professor of German, she was a flautist.
The combustion lasted well into the evening,
then even as the spirit that came tumbling from
the eyes was ever new, was changed with what
I think could not come later. The relaxation
was again very serious and prefaced the world
as well as the other, for which we were so pre-
ternaturally grateful that we put our shoes on
once again and decided to leave. She was a sis-
ter to the king. I could have been taking pic-
tures this whole time. In fact I was, but only
with the small window that was left stranded
near a dock that struggled with what it was. It
hated the ocean, which it rarely opened its eyes
to see. Thus I'm not sure of what I came away
with a record of. Now it's true that these chil-
dren, of whom I certainly have images locked
in memory, have faces that could not straggle
toward an alternate eclipse. I should look back
later, when there will be a better chance of see-
ing the whole picture. There is a man, too,
somewhere none of us expects. He sits in front
of us, but with us, no more inhibition to dia-
gram than a frog or horse. Of Paris, knowing

to write about the worst of the worst, which is
not even that. Which is the thing if one were
to inhale it there would be a conquering. Need
you know what I am saying? Need I? How
many sheets of unbelievable knowing go to-
ward what you're building? How many parks
are in front of you, hovering, masking, trail-
ing? Your feet orchestrate what we've always
heard. They cancel the interferences, which are
all that matter, since they have an obverse ob-
ject. Most battles with the world are just now
in Paris. It takes recent cities seriously but ends
up at the last second leaving.—Is there any way
Paris is here now? I'm not sure it's fun to be-
lieve those sensations, in their immediateness,
in their saying. They should have been about
another layer of building block, any sediment,
another rudimentary habitat. They should have
lunged out of embarrassment, to notice the
broad outlines, to subject their own tribe to
questioning. No matter what should have hap-
pened it was enough, no matter what I said,
even the markup of random syllables, I wanted
something to mean something else, I wanted
something—to—be—heard. We don't under-
stand French very well, strict inventions, lost
context. What if Paris were here, since most of
what I do is think of you, lost place, like any
place lost, or any contest that is mind only. Any
abandoned solidity, any caravan you choose.

Having been here: if that was not the case then awful companies would feature our knowledge. But that was not to be. We were we. How can so many cities be planned to deny it? Where you live must be nothing to where you are. A handful of medicated surgeons. So many dice. Who dwelt, who were disabled, aggrandized, birthed. Nothing within that solid frame made solidity come. Only when jet exhaust maneuvered yet again. To be. Only when jet exhaust began to coat the receptors, as it happened the waist-high rumors, arms restrained and movies brought to light. With filters nothing will come true. Sitting in a heat-enacted futuristic tube, how will we recalcify, how will numbers raise a frame. The scotch of destinations kept us from our scopes. If it were drunk then a cameraman would wonder at its frost, its light, and shapes that could come through. And how we center, what instances our awful blue. If chance is what is labeled then what are we to do? Sense can be the worst for us, awful in its looking new. And irony. Bending the filmic instances quiver like nothing new. Absences burn in this forward what we view. The nationhood of lingering, the saintliness of rice. Delete on delectation in remembering advice. Or so true, the marks that trembled on a grid, the grid that trembled to be marked. Did someone function in a nearer light? Who is awake now? Transposed and censored by the fight. I've never refused. I've always refused. I'll die to make more sense of now, the razor and the light capturing a hand about a quarter the size of mine. I'm letting go and going back to feeling able again. No more lengthy talk of rights. The shorn engulfing repurposes, our magnates tell us they are rich. There must be no one left to message this. As if a whisper to itself rejects. As if a well a spear of grass rejects a game, triumph over humanity. If then the game, if then the play resulting in reprieve, still there's an end, precisely that imagined. Even if I'd gone strictly multidirectionally away from you, even with no legs I was concomitant and held forward like a bristle in forgeries, and walking on the moon, and drying in the sun, lackluster cinemas holding an ancient rhyme. Every time I bless you I get to know you better, wanting to bless you is the same as an enclosure, having been taught the word, having been brought up. How do I look in the mirror, or how am I supposed to match what you said? We chose flights that would be just as flawless if the ground swelled beyond them, if the marches shut them down. Just as obvious, I fill a decanter with your idiolects, not for an instant feeling bad. I was the same as wax, but the candies looked like the flagpoles, and the pollen worked its way up to the top. All manner of brides deter-

mined the future, wherewithal revised into a
canticle of mirth. If torpedoes were shucked
they can't have behaved well, if behaviors up-
loaded your impact then I wish you well. And
to wish you the best is like the lunar fixation, a
limerick cold against the commonality of luck.
I would balloon, I would come back, I would
sing, as a forward progression, limber shall be a
field, halo contact, hands on hips. I know it
was foretold, was found, was freed after felt as
if feltro were found after all. Why do I remem-
ber that name, why is magnitude mysterious
like mountains and men? Oh labyrinth for-
ward from which I love, is there an aerial view?
I'm listless like a minotaur all built up like a
man. In labor was I born but now born with
lostness, nothing much to do, too much any-
way. Follow the sword, or the candle, or the
mixed appropriation in the swale. And inevita-
ble, the performance through which I've
searched and dreamt, perhaps no one you've
ever seen before. And sealed, the contract al-
lowing interference by the expunged, even one
instance a martyred instance. And to repeal,
what had we needed to say? My suggestion was
to go formulaically to the office, to discuss.
What I was was such a distant relation to what
was in place that a severity of treatment
rounded out an endgame, a natural center fi-
nally found. The cranes on the periphery never

ceased on 42nd street, as if anywhere they ceased. What about what was home? If I were in one of the holes that surround us, would sight result, a kind of mole, embattled, tiny, given an example of ground that had to satiate itself or not take anything in at all? Even if I were to remember my own life, would that still be a waste? There is a chord that plays constantly, its one long note wrapping about our minds until a tide in effect lifted the long intense boats. My conception was equally present, my cancer was nowhere heard. How often lies are spoken depends entirely on who is left, who negates the frailest of them. Then, then, what ends up being complete remains in the quarter hold, a tank in which floats what we said. That factor was in a bright real position, until a ceremony felt noticeable. When would you have said the potential for feedback was measured on the index billboard? I suggest that "why not"'s categories are broader than a military, that my shields and your shields are just shields and cages have uses, leave them alone. Ceremony is holiday anyway so try the bright version. Was it true that I wrote more when I wrote less? I wagered several thousand dollars. I was more than fine, I leapt suddenly without a jacket into the conclusion, into the wish. And how did he make it there, strange slats pried off one another, which took so much time? The reverse idea was better than the first one, no heat working its way up the neck before we were able to stop spending. We took the ideas and put them together by the look of the ends of their openings, their feet as it were. When this version of a slight arrival became a treetop, that was our verb for descend. I've ignored the words of the last thousand years, 1,000 up to about now. Every time I wasn't going to say something I believed in God once more. My arms plump with air, I am once again with you, after a day of being with you, the new shape of fatherhood near a hotel pool in the sun with a girl who is me on a wave she could not fall into. What did we say about what we could possibly come into, how much could we gamble in one day? A siege takes place against what you might think. It's stowed away in there. Our floating away with each word, a corsage of sorts looking repeatedly from a pupil's window, questions of his making a moment eternal, separate, and genuine. Awful sitting to wait for the angel of invention to attend feelings that not once have come up before. Each piece of the celebration was memorable and beyond monetary value. I have recoiled from holding hands with my son. I have been home enough to know how much I'm missing. Any discreet moment has its eternity. You've missed a thousand of your own. We'll make up the time before our final destination. Until then capture a purity of sight. One word more. The stumbling block was placed there by a massive number of parties, scratching the surface of Tier 2 tasteful agreements. I'm worried that our corner room will be missing even the arti-facts listed on the receipt, which once had their own burdened faces but now encapsulate typo-graphic appendages, unfurled, unraveled, with a global purpose. (Any two boards will go to-gether with the right combination of words be-hind and in front of them.) Still the battles are waged identically, the party dresses are laid out around the living room on furniture large enough to be brought in through the midget doorways. And still, arguing without purpose (I think) we look like authentic Greeks only as a result of a vapid biology. Soon the cornucopia of psychotropic inferences will harvest total factions of best abilities (the fewer words I use the fewer of them I'll have, and vice versa). Ab-horred by a factional market we get a pure boost from a morning soda. There is little else but soda, even if we refuse to admit it, turning coastal things against the until-now straight-ened method of warping ourselves into faked journeys or worked-against militant innocent fabulists. It takes only three words to dispel (quagmire!) the tube through which one might yell at the others but through which enough light passes that little tableaus are available to look at. No one seems to be holding out over there. Everyone on this train is substantially interested in waiting. An American prince, as in the book for young readers. He comes over for lunch. Even with the multiple recurring nightmares we were still impressed. Even with the costly bridge giving way, its scribe just another scribe. After we ate, we held up our shields and practiced declaring a truce. How sillily ornate of us, to want to see the body in such a spasm. No two insights led to the same conclusion, though when we got to the last section of this particular group of waking hours we could trace in the nightgown what happened and whose drawer things belonged in. No one exists who does not have a range of possibilities, trucks from around the world have their past mentions. The path is a mold that no one is paid to service. It should have been better than this but let's not get too involved. Metal sheets stick together for most people and there's no reason not to emerge from other insights. If you are you . . . Well, again, I'd like to suggest we vote and call it a day, get back on the bus, roll on home. It's the same piece of land whether it's drawn as creek or as trumpet. True, different brands of corruption will be tallied, but the current atmosphere shields us from those difficulties. He's camouflaged perfectly for those grasses. Only an idiot would approach a potential detonation like that (and boy was he a bald-headed idiot!). Pontifical infusions will always be good enough. It's a dress code. It's a third-degree literacy. It's a landing or an imaginary island where supplies are brought in by the catty. Me and you, we can do something about this. We can look right to each other and foster such combatants that everyone will be proud. Each institution has its own flag. There's a polygraph that helps us intuit who was there. With an extreme rendering of makeover services, it was surprising that the mechanic was such a nice guy. In the middle of church, we decided to stand up and dance, but we quickly realized that what we were doing was embarrassing for most everybody and we returned to our seats to pray again. Voting is not as fragmented as it looks yet certain features of your interests will not be acknowledged. The stereoscopic tincture of broadband release is wrapped up, if not warmed over, by whatever clouds are scheduled for that day. Letters look priceless in the right light, though oftentimes they seem lost in their own ambition. They are brash intrusions, shave with a knife, every time they find a family there's another commercial break, thematics replaced before the continuance of regular programming. If everything was lost then of course we're still left with everything, broken and brand new in leisure. Shifty-eyed salesman comes to dinner more than once. In fact, your tornado intimacy brightly corresponds. In fact, what's one more day? I can say that polecats are like return tickets, eardrums have spokes, cable cars look antiquated, but they are who they are. I completely appreciate bananas on bread. Weeping as we read the *Economist*, we're still snazzy, we're still savvy with each other. It's the same thing as a terminus. Peace talks are genuine, but not the need you've meandered into the specialty shop with. Now at the flummoxed internment of birth thoughts, navigators look like they want to take classes. Lobotomy is an option but I'll wait for the others to make that decision for me. I was sitting and suddenly there was nowhere else for us to stand. Its shaved head distracted us, but its wig was like the crown of an infant king. I'm supposed to be reading this, not hurling insults. I was part of a determined breeze that collided with a rooftop then got human, looking respectable at all times but then so clenched with importuned language that there was a question of lasting, a moment the whole group was anticipating and thinking of writing about afterward. Still, facades often change quickly sometimes even as part of a plan. Still, no one else participated or looked west. The books themselves were stunning examples of watchtowers and of course looking-glasses. No two of the conditions looked like they had been through the same training seminar. Oh, I know, shave your head and get to the top, but somebody has to be an illustration of frankness. There is no possible way to posit a block of text, as if it were coming off an assembly line in Detroit. That's impossible. Then, if you have sex with someone else, I hope your joy was not black in its wing. Else this ink will fall against the same exclusion. This is not the interior of my palm, likened to a flower's flesh, but a series of old and invisible interactions that themselves exhibited this potential for prediction. Enough, tea duets lack their erstwhile lacustrine infringements. Now, by a dim evening bulb, weaving happens even by the forgetful, now I will accept nothing but the epic of sheetrock & hushed earth tones. And Wednesday, when the conclusion hits, paradigms elapse and suddenly your face hurts, cognizing its intimate mistakes. *Still* we're barbecuing with the fumes getting in the neighbors' saris. This is not inaction or its implicit action, but a biography of dwarves and common-sense handwriting. Your change may have been lost on the magic plateau. Just imagine if they grew up without public television, clean bathrooms, awkward looks over the expanse of what they never were. To have had you in mind, for that morning, shimmering at the other's elbow. They should have been ashamed, tsunamis of copied reality. Even the insouciance, which in the man with the shaved head counts for little since it's the counterpoint technique of petting an eyeful of the girl. But any of us would know, if shuffling alone, masters of blight. Crowds that have taken longer than I exist in the road it seems I'm first to reach. How hidden behind language can one possibly be. How is this a poem and that not a poem and that shored up against becoming precisely this, which in conscious choice and darkness points to an unfilled participant? I am not mourning, but enumerating. I hope in your work as well an expression of society's ontological failure to capture human energy is papered against a thin mist. There is a bulk of poorly hidden waste material. If not there then somewhere in the slim country, in the "later" during which "sense" doesn't compromise its intelligence. A portrait is like an idle audience participant. You may get turned into your own narrowness, your own blizzard of alternate levers and polecats drifting against underbrush. Last night, in any case, there was not the tiniest glimmer of the workaday world, which today has again begun to function. Lightning itself is conveyed in a tenuous arc across the sky, we fathom it by looking directly up. What strikes me is that the burden is so slim. That is exactly what we'd planned, dramatic entrances knocking the hosts off balance, if we could. Then at some point the situation with the boy changed, for one thing he combed his hair. Dear anyone, I have lusted after you once again. The drainage canals are now overflowing, you see, misplaced larger detritus creating impassable perspectives of liquefaction. It's great to be back, even without my heavier coat. My skin and its eyes gaze and breathe, gaze and breathe a savage localness, indications of their old labors making landscapes tenable and new. A barrage of hurrah, just like last time. Every time I think of you I want to get back in the car. Dear highway traffic, I know you'll be here longer than me. And dear solstice, the road away from you is like a teenager, making up his mind. Don't tell the audience what indications to look for, what corner of a screen kept its place, a large-scale pacing. Now, back at the campsite, a gargantuan room has risen over the meadow. I'm surprised by the amount of light reflected in the shimmering grasses, which are audible in their brushing against each other. The sky is dark, dead altitude, its native land this far from city light. I'm certain I've articulated this diaphanous pricelessness, cognition unjustly prioritized. You're shooting yourself in the foot by not defining the situation. You're agog with stereological manufacture and even an ice cream won't help, even your own thick come-uppance, based in a pilot light. A given morning is a given morning. Let's remember: this cell contains an equation based on other cells, other worksheets. If you walk away from what you are doing, one notices. Have a cookie. Your resultant aesthetic dribble will commence. Fairy flowers and fairy lights are on my hands, which let go if the anything approaches my lips. What results from these stretches of time is rather unusual, though consistent with deep injury. She should have decided by now, but we forgive her. There is nothing so quiet as a single light somewhere, nothing so quiet as you, as a car parking in front of the house, as consistency itself, on a round operating table, a mosaic of wood dining-room tables peppering the neighborhood as possible energy, as adjustments on the agenda, as mistakes in terminology, as secret burials of fish. Ultimate ideas were voted into place then revised, as quiet as trouble, which is the force of order, which stepped outside, is crushing, human body magnifying its surface area by spreading out invisibly, in the way of force, a golden delicious tossed in the spice isle, then a spat ensuing, dusting up an already ruffled feather, quieted by managers who take thousands of dollars plus the stony home, where we follow them, where you should know a dumbbell rings that would not have otherwise been heard. Tension of sand. Whoever's words you were. Suburban tension a luggage for you, a comic inscape of good fortune, spelled out then guessed. My ignorance has stunned both of us, even *with* the candy you look for someone else. Did she tell you? I think so. Did management say so? I think that yesterday they were the same people. When I get an email from an officeholder I always say yes, or get out and do something real. That's when it first leaps out, every last word possibly said at that absurd moment, interlinked events and all I was thinking about was failure. At just that genuine blueness we performed our dispute, both going far over the speed limit down the neighborhood highway we subsidized, even without the bridge we expected over the Laundromat. I was expecting a veto but the bill stayed in the senate, every citizen having a mind to put their hand to the cold cement. And perhaps that was about it, credit card receipts lifted by the approaching new hurricane. I'm against the skyscraper skein. What showed outside of only those bra straps we were looking for was the heavy drum that would simply have to be replaced. I'm sure there's much thinking going on in there, but at the heart of each of us is a kind of Tyco severity. Surely, nothing plastic spared, nothing not caught in the gamma of romance or function of payment, not this week at least. As tall as you are, you won't see over the iron claws of the staged entrapment you tripped over on your way to the filing cabinet, you won't contract the boot camp by yelling, or sway in the academic breeze like the rebuttals whose countless odors you've processed. If you read purpose into savory intelligence I'd like to ask what gimmick palliatives give the best return. I was looking for something I could hedge against. The story was a reprimand, a palliative swinging and fighting for its life, unable to forget a kind of motivational substance. Why win anything? If nothing will change afterward? If I have a thought it's of not being able to walk, it's of the side of a working relationship that's a singular talking vs. rolling over. I want to change the functioning of my judgment, before it's so early that we realize a panoply of silt and minor effluents, void in many ways of the girl, who in Yemen was hidden well. Exactly right that the corrosion was written out not only on your bedroom wall but in exclusive engagements the cognition of which would have been nice since then at least the gossip tree could have favored ignorance. Certainly there are few requirements for inclusion in the meandering creek beds, perhaps rolling in from a dry extreme hillock is a primrose path. To smell what's arranged itself is to know the hard morsels of construction. But cable news looks at how we're not building at the most extreme heights, which must be a victory for realistic action, I mean since the order of the community is at stake. A new rate structure, as if I could search for something. At birth with sin we're given ends, then with bodily growth we conceive minds, almost immediately. The therapist goes back in time to help us reply to original queries, a painful road that likens itself to either class failure or monolinguisitic rebellion. I know everything, you're given rock lyrics. Pacing the labeling, Canada coming down, out of pure compassion, the lick piercing postal attires. Indeed, there was no way to remove the tree without digging up the whole house, and finally we allowed it to grow somewhere else. Sludge. I guess it would be now, for that. Rumors hit against the beach like even-keeled frigates taken with their own comfort. Psychological bliss has to do with not thinking of what might happen. And seeing the world is yet another lesson, as if we heard a song approaching and decided it belonged to someone else, a Narcissus, or a defender of the faith. It was when in the evening light we yet again say "down to dinner" that I realized I needed to change language itself, to hide what I knew of it in the open closet and propose alternatives. Your presence in the museum would be detailed over the next few years, captured lead-time banging its head, counting to five the number of victims who have fallen from this same rock, into the rapids of this proverbially beautiful place. I *am* an architect, just like the others. But with me the commission is motionless, brought to bear like a bizarre shade inhabiting a place from which no one imagined a return. It was me you were looking for. Then it was yourself, I was you, a car drones by with an ad for family photographs on top, entrapment like a wound antilinguisticly screaming from the barren clean faces. Excitement and sludge are true enemies, except when thrown together. They designate what happens to prelates controlling the tides. Smoke the cigarette, tear strips from the banner to make baby banners, the near analyses releasing several emotions at once. At my suggestion, stemming from my interrogation, historic filtering we had cheap technology for. Pinning hopes on recycled paper is like looking at a plastic runway during a parade. There's so much time for a judgment that even the bobcats are found looking through garbage. There is no other insistence scheduled in the morning precinct. Savor what you can. The magazine looks and feels like an apple skin. I'm in charge of looking it over. I've come to realize that touch will reveal more than words. A dream revolves like a carousel, exit when you wish. Rings are there if you are fast enough to take them. When exiting, hand them to the functional attendant, the one at the concession stand that does not accept cash. I promise not to be so sober any more. That's no way to win you back, that's a tree that forks about itself like an early modern sculpture. If you'll remember, as birds we landed on it. With little texture on its surface we kept losing our grip. No doubt we had to go, back to the infantry, back to the contractual tease I care about. But really, what it indicates is a safe recognition, or something in blue-brown, glossed over as if coated in tears. Soon we'll be parsing out what we know of what we wanted. It's up to others to fill in the gaps. I've forgotten what I was saying. I've been holding out in terms of what I was going to do with the correct meaning. I'm fairly certain you helped me proceed in the right direction but that least suited the realities of my background. Certainly a number of holiday caves lasted the entire course of my compassions. Hush, I hear the train coming. It presages nothing for the surrounding brush. Well, no single stem lasts a year, bargains last just a day. Change, like a complete sky, never "happens" in context. Only with the caution of false perspectives, ladders no one understands. Text is never traced by a finger, which only surrounds it and is part of its light. My rites were lost one day as I got knocked over by a wave. Related to its incompletion. I'm not sure where you've taken me. Vision is like a body in itself. If learning to dance, then shift your burden away from where you are, a position of dominance. Probably 30% of being here is shunning away, the other 70% not knowing who is behind one. Repeating mystery, or regarding it. I would like a response. I would reprise the devolution of the partitions, how our city took its name. Anyway, I'm in the same car, in the mid-80s. His car is there, off to the side. He shifts so his son's head rests on the pillow next to him, instead of on his shoulder. I'm not sure anything can be found in the self, or in the self's replication. She came over to our site about the time the veil was pulled over the chimney, seclusion exchanging places with the tried and true. With less and less interest I read the debate, a labored breathing. Tonight there's a line in the forest that leads back in time. Moments before we sleep one equivalent was the moment before we decided to go. The look of what you are doing is not as bad as its concrete outcome. There is nothing about you that is not you, if indeed I sensed who you were. My chain of results tells me the location, but I know it's what you've wanted all along. But whatever circumference of a circle spirit won't do, such that the ascetic way proves true. But all of it came down at once, the fragments of the remaining tropes, the highways of fearing reversed time. One idea of time is that it reverses the normal course of events, like digging a hole as a prelude to major construction, or like a master plan rolled up into a tight ball. Every one of the thresholds you mentioned turned unbridgeable. We settled in but the sting of return, the giant spectrum, the causes trickled down the outlines until they separated and became waterfalls. If I had studied for the exam I would have felt better. I would have acknowledged the scientific reduction I had been bred to combat. If I had slept well last night, if I had sundered my in situ, the circumscription might have been lighter, less round. Instead it surged & we generated tractates as if we were decades younger. We fell, we rose, we dressed as warmly as we could. We limped to the finish line with skates in our hands. I was ready though I was sitting in my flat reading your letter. It looked like a dream crossing a shelf. Seated in a fortress carved in an overhang, we repelled down to a dangerous sea. Once down, we went back up, we went to the right and the left, we repented the signature of previous hours, we shunned the inclusion of ladders of rope. Deeds get done, and that's what I did, echoes coming from a wooden box, collective unconscious forming like a forest floor or a latter day saint. Sand comes to us equally, if we figure it out, if we let it get us in trouble. Wish lists included coverlets from popular stores. One gainful expectation followed another. It then matters how you're expected to calculate the expectation, which was explained but forgotten. Held aloft it echoes against an argument to keep still, or responds to increases in openings. Sentences determine what comes after, as I've said again and again. My glad environment was portioned out like teeth against a faint bland toothsomeness. There was never one swig of beer. Shimmering perfectly, my memory could not be clearer, my thought stands alone. Even if you were manufacturing a clause it would search-beam buried treasures, basic comments of telling each other near-truths. It was a day that turned backward, then pieced together what it saw very quickly. Non sequitor an escape from cliché. Buried against each other I'm not sure I can rest. My miracle is getting up for water, my waste is dreaming what never happened. The strategic breaching of who is not there. One day again in fifteen years I'll be a blade of grass as now. What we'd said was very quiet, almost nonexistent, which burdened our awkward beginning or flight.

How little that flight matters: I trace the recurrent wondering to its source. I have come back to this wage. Wish never being there, it became a test for what was possible. But who could compete with you, who among the genuine would have knowledge of the center of light? In its first lead there was innocence, when with sure selves we stumbled over actual images, the search for a landscape took charge. To be forced across a blue insensitive ship, no other achievements representing our capture. I'm not sure what limpidness you had seen, but there it was. Backward, or at least different. Scraped away, we found the errant flakes of ourselves and kept them in a pointed opaque jar. Scrape along then. Let light, first light in. Any nonaction and the active will flee. They presupposed the fortunate prospect that led back to the beach. I took Wednesday off but was strange about winter. It was like looking through something I'd originally missed. How many more sudden crests could be slipped in, or, anyway, how many capsules resembled slings containing arrows containing outrageous. I terminate a passive week and promote a favorite winking. Paroxysms don't matter, neither does touch. Quite a few people are not looking for a good time. Quite awkward once more in the unusual stage of deterioration, when the lineages pursue what was asked and the novice accompanists are generally limber. Even as the imaginary line with the format the prospectors encountered in dust. Not responding to the crop of adherents, today's, yesterday's, who can say when. If one more word from me appears, then that is something new. That serves beyond question as an exact replica of before we took each other into the grateful rebounding percentage that looked inward, looked to be a finishing touch. I'm stuck with intense feeling, I'm ashamed to resurface near the waves. Whose burning is it to retrieve that, to wonder at its exactitude. Just when repetition did not matter, we juggled continuous creating until worship was like a glove. And extreme foreshadowing was slept through, able academics and hopeful grudges, and how I can see, and how tell. One summer another summer took its place, another altitude flew into view. He was the one implied in the sentencing, the debt acting as mate, acting as praise. Mathematics looks like a green star, or like institution whisking across the surface of a shell. Sorry, but that really makes me feel bad! Makes me wish there were more chairs around here. If there was only enough space we could bring back absolutely everything, we could decline to resist the functioning of the limber tribes, we could step up and reward the inhabitants with abandoned fuselages, with cookies and milk. And when there was no effort at remembering the sly salute was guaranteed, that posture lent us its lilt. And to be stuck on the inhabitants was like a privileged exchange, like removing the wings from a bird. I would have to comply but the rewards would be worth it. I would have to move south and return north each day at cost. Still, don't make a fuss or we'll be brimming over with sweat. No one else could participate in the strange habits, or the weary looks of centuries keeping watch. Time, the balm, refused to go on the trip with us, it labored like an ecclesiastical garnish. It was supposed to have run into a fountain with its car, its notions were splashed, it got to the point where it had to lick humor from a crevice or two, grime not always a cancerous antipode. The cereal first, then the milk. If more of the lucky folks were on vacation, I could stare down that hypothesis until it came true. Around the table were the hearts I was constructed of, later I'll find out how that made a difference. We send our bodies over the hill of chance, then as a smile is redeemed a shade is drawn against recovering languages. Its "might" was frequently "might," some said nothing and lived to constitute society and look nice, talk nice, behave. If against the shutters a soldierly mass alights, if repeating shoulders, if caps take flight, suggestiveness. Liter-

ariness. Who was, was. Stop and shop. Driving
through the purchases of only twenty years
ago, we beckoned to another complex of deci-
sions, seemed fine, then swallowed excessive
bits. There is no other color but white, for
malls anyway. There is no research I can fight,
behind the yellow line. Swine, they puncture
mind with their snouts. Hey, like most men.
And would that not be enough to excuse the
embarrassment that shaped our good occasion?
I was the only one who knew that no one's
story was more perfect than yours. How be-
come, fall back, when achieved, able again to
arrive, when lost among the pages. And when
terrific moments cave in across the dreams re-
worked, when you could you did. And at last
an engagement posited, removed, lifted like
air. Last night I got in the car and drove south
past San Jose. Positive force sobs back after skin
it replaces. Ordinary busts look blue except I
can see, from my incline, what was at stake,
gemlike, in my past, near the knoll where we
lay. She concluded with a hug. This week ev-
eryone shipped Friday, looked like tangled sto-
ries blocked out against what was said, as in de-
termined workhorses. You knock against the
window every day, but who will outlast that
category? She didn't say we should think strong
thoughts. She never managed to talk about se-
quences. She never included a lasting sym-

phony of tower bells, sober chimes even weeks ahead of time. And she said "who" could lift "that face" up, except a lake, a change like a ladder, left in a quarry? It says a lot about who is thinking about this, who is grouped together with a satellite box, or a shell arresting its wan watering. How long can one work for a library? It matters later, when one is placed against a rock. It looks like a light but don't be a fool. If you are in there then there's an issue with conscious truth. With a Jamesian fortitude and an excessive pride, the delight of day is a thin ice cream. Even at a remove your corner of engagement lights the sky. Then you realize this brood is someone else's. That was a book that should not have been pursued. A moving in my mouth, stage of the extreme edge. I'm falling to, moving hands and feet, the screed is adjusted forward. Sensate is the same as sense. Genuine flattery is still genuine. What creates my mouth is a nearness of now and of happening now. Chains grab at least some of us, not least others. Notes tell at least part of the story, at risk for sending everything away. Sly betrayals account for what my eyes do. They summon me to what's waiting but that's screened off. Diligent languages look the same as temporary housing, as charges of velocity encoded by a freak. Probably the body could link to its own source. It could break countless natures and still be one, count its pores and still perch in its own tree. If you saw your tree you might know. Leaves fall quickly but they recover equally well. Finally most branches fall away, and it is this lesson that sits with us the longest. She took most of that with her when she died. We're looking at the video even now, coadvanced as it could possibly be. Against that epoch, what are we? A sestina done at dinner with a sonneteer, a mostly faith-inspired looker-on. "B is the shape of," that's the phrase I was looking for. Any language can have its way, the way I've come about, particulars in the feeding. Its ceremony is its value, after that only shifts and falls. As, at risk of maturing, my mouth ascends to the last town. What should we have done, like broken trees? What phantasm sat there radioing? With purposeful suction and inanimate glee our factions lanced their compunctions. They had organized and would say much the same thing. It ages, but not severely not as awkwardly as one had thought. Norway is the poetic equivalent of managed competition. Tears formed wrinkles and vice versa. The sublime is like a constituent who keeps summarizing the volunteers. There were a range of volunteer pilots, there were freight cars and fritters. Magnitudes of apple pie, force fields of grass, of schoolhouse will. If I were to age I'm not sure I could look the same, not sure of brain or revenge. They are the same as a charge out of the woods, horses rearing against torn branches. If I were to speak I could age, I could resist, possibly crumble, but still look like a white wall, a rebarbative cornerstone pinioned in sludge. I'm not sure anyone else has taken notes, which is why devices are true. At each stage I concluded that I was being artistic. But none of the rills waited to look at me again. No one else needs to document the flood, the lost have become friends, swell friends. Someone registered a Safeway in my name, I started an airline by fashioning a stilt. I don't think anyone would have needed to know. As far as parades go you're like an antiparade, you're a serial perturbation of a shoe. Some tribes shovel this landscape for millennia. That's not possible any more their descendants are still here. They talk about the old ways but none of it *really* makes any sense. We're consumed by a feeling of loss, but early predictions come closer to whatever courses through our veins. Toward the same institutional breath I want to scatter the filaments bunched in my breast. Arrangements have the same attraction as a host of laborers. Frank's filaments were legion, but not his constitution. Aging was just an idea. How many places do I need to keep? The strange list from localization, the headweary, and the ownership. As if struck from the mill, ordered off the deck, segmented and aware. What am I looking for? Am expunging influence, a break off but then a break in, a force that looks like what it says. Even in duties, bored in what was ahead, we captured the red lining and let the focus shift. It depends on whose sharing is routine, it strikes out but covers its pendulum with a shock of loam. Until we're dead we think "there's no trouble thinking." It streams out of its corrugated temple, the latest in ornithological closeness. Lingering across roofs, cardigans beneath the lightest tents. Who could look further than this but you? I looked at it and found quite a few ways to define it. Lapsed language, sure, but not a set of tires. Your portrait is placed against a facade of stone. It's the same poem again, willed amnesia. How can I come back over to what you were? We weren't doing *anything* else, no more than straying across the isle, to the purveyors of contrariness. Baffle the best only, keep on. That frozen oscillation, that contemplative stricture, comatose. It's just how I am me. Makes no difference. Makes no prepared frozenness, not officially, not blatant in the clean isle. This manner of stating the obvious was a staggering affront. Look how little is getting done. The concept is like lines in a parking lot. The other concept is like jigging in place. Are you weary yet, or have you posed a question? Fortune will look at you just as you look at it. Like a management trainee. How many chairs were there? The lighting wasn't right. The humor was impolite. Thanks for coming out in this weather. I think the proprietor was shelving travel books during the reading. The former poet laureate was encased in what he was. Was there something we knew? All she could be was her dual loves, all she could speak of, write about. Poetry was no longer something in the room. A gloom from Poe or some nineteenth century arrival made me want to leave. What he spoke of was how we are in our postcreative solace. There was someone outside the bookstore who had all the marketing slapped out of them. But seriously, I agreed with the men who were nodding assent. At lighter moments during one day after another he would look distraught, though by noontime he'd accept queries. The life I imagined at the break between stanzas in the long poem about the creation of the poem. I finished counting chains at the same time as the old cradle fell. I think it was well-attended though poorly introduced. Then too the structure fell apart at the end when the last poet jolted from the podium and left an expectation of seeing the bookstore attendant smile and say goodnight. California grasses trouble the eyes. No shape could match theirs. No one has any enthusiasm left. The pink tongue hides in the

weeping mouth. Everybody has their pearly
whites, their charred remains. The dislocated
glove was up next. It looked like a sheen and
spoke warmly. My two fingers in my wife's
hand were the stillness of my efforts. None of
the people who felt like singing decided to
speak. The business end of an entrepreneurial
sex-find, grudges agglomerate then structure
then resist. The pinpoint rhythm has nothing
to do with relief. Finally, after your father in-
stilled the enthusiasm, there was no more than
absorbing tripartite speech patterns. The look
and the voice were at angles to the person be-
tween us. Suggestion slips filled the tiny card-
board boxes. There's something obvious about
the whole enterprise, but no one knows what it
is. Your desperate problem keeps the moments
away, as supplied by a blinking eye, as cali-
brated by an unanswered question that by a
single look by a single person was answered
with a look. If the water is not supposed to be
there, then who is? People are each other, and
it is up to us to feel like we have no minds. If
you are a bracket of ash, then I am a time zone
that comes after you. If you are a matrix of
longing, then I am a requirement laid to rest. It
looks bizarre. I am in charge of manufacturing
the appropriate map, or at least of a mimesis of
thoughtlessness. A great game as suitable win-
ter coat. Who could have been there for us,

when we'd left so many behind? Cost was a shaky model. The elephant in the room was the humanities, our mission to turn them toward a sea of white. Foundational hypotheses are dubious, but look at all this automaticity. She jingles back and forth those keys in the hard hat. You're not permitted to listen to the gravelly voice. A kiss that happens in a vehicle is interesting. The universe does have a negative, but only because things seem to need to disappear. The outcome was predictable, but only to those who were willing. If only to notify the people in the upper tiers, the organizers and affordability parties. If only to have counted right or just counted. Often the signs knelt at slightest provocation at the first stage of trying to penetrate their mass. A whole city might be more inclined to whistle with you, might be lighter than our least effort, which was reproduced under a range of conditions. Most of the elements of choruses are fake but they gather a sincerity over the course of a performance. Then each chorister reverts to being a mere chime in a desert wind. If you watch yourself roll down a hill you might understand the undue pigment or the parrying. Organs populate the handiwork, lifelines do not count. To behave differently is a tier that miniscule opportunities rush. With little possibility of taking suggestions, nominal archives make their own sense. Speaking is behaving, speak differently. Ordered sun comes here. Cast across the waters we live near, ocean, bay, streams, various pools, it's the same way we live. Often a gentleness will result, poetry a banana. Often, your hobby located beneath a layer of distaste, there is little left for the ages we've become, subtle epoch-continuing chapters. I want only to return to our first peace, to give my big presentation, in an almost unconscious remainder. Another body of water was Jewel lake. We should have stayed in that one spot, on the opposite shore from the blue heron. Nothing moved, but nothing was paid to move. The sun gave that one thing remove, talons curved around thefts of dried marshweed. If only you could say, once your festival ended, that this was real. The conspicuous hopefuls in the tube. Air does not matter here. Symphonies may play, but air escapes again. If an Arab goes knocking, then who will play cello, or if a rock flies across a public square, who catches it? The subgenre of pulled pork liquefies the rope. What other look would mean returning here, except the one I searched for all alone? Behave, face flat against a billboard, pressed by a palm in every other place. What if I caught fire or fell from a lamppost strangely out of place? Nothing is not a question, nothing is not an erstwhile answer. He is

strategic in his calm routine, the excess of its
rust. The shared corners of his Blackberry, the
conjugal musts, the aped routine. To whom
does lyric matter, or why can we live together,
structure of suggestion and unrevealed stria-
tions of rock. Who cares? Who can salute? I'm
not sure who else I have killed, or stilled, for a
very long time. They will adhere, minor pas-
sages and new ways of looking included in a
shoebox. Shapes of professionals linger near
our house, they cobble their nearness, cobble
their height. To have an arm, then slide our
right legs back. I'm not sure who is involved. If
you travel incessantly something must be right.
If you overtake the limestone, that's a way to
light. They've accomplished what no other
remnant could, the building of temples and
homelands no research remembered, or the
spiny similitude of forests uninhabited, small
accountings of peace. If he were surrounded by
paper then no disenfranchisement, no one in
hunger would come to his door. A manic ele-
gance served as love, then his ship was disman-
tled in shallow Bangladesh. How about that? A
good feel. As the razors are flowery and tumble
to the river. It must have been planned, or a
fashion statement or a wandering into danger-
ous territory. Personally I like the inhibitors of
the dead zone, or a walrus tank, or a ship to
shore abstraction. But you know what I like,

personally. Sugar on top, braised lamb, a zodiac outlined in pinholes on a salmon cake. Last week I delighted in a barbarous code, and I related to the family gathering as I would to the eye of London. It merged with other ideas. It gently lost all of its air. The stage was a journey in and of itself. No one remembered how to jettison our particular failsafe wagon wheels, but ethereally we knew how to behave. No scenery was reached, except for what was referred to by lifting our hands flat against any gaze. Not many of the war years looked as good as this one. Jogging away, prehistoric flight, there was one thing personal in the baby pictures posted to the back of the van. Every epic target, it so happens, every caryatid was a girl I knew. If wind can make you change course, who else controls you? Certainly no one looks like they're waiting for instructions. Several gentle faces come up with requests, fresh looks, faded underwear. Then recent animals are searched, achievements are the same as whistles, burgundy bargains and labeled bracelets; how, without a body, can she know? I'm sure the preserved light will capsize, that no one has designed it, and no one should. From above, the houses looked like haloes, then charms tucked under patriotic lampshades. If burned by light, posit alternate homegrown saviors, red hair and teeth the size of toenails. If fortune were a frown or an absence, I would take it lightly, I would become less able, during an investigation. They conducted a focused search for its outline. The strategic bitmapping became its most mature aspect, as if we had our minds ready. One is excused in face of unknown revelations near the Canadian shore. Solidity was a factor outside of the less recent objects. They saved their idea of surface for change agents, they are glued to what it amounted to before the rebels said otherwise. I am successful at saying things, a snail savior. Order appreciates me then moves along. He hides and is never hidden again. Swords and other weapons in the mix, thinking their way through things. Inhabit habit, instruction par excellence, as if an order by progression were in a seat next to mine. No these are those who rest, even during the annunciation, oh the ready if bad poems at the middle of the volume. I forget how I knew her, but it was love at first sight. I enjoyed that stage then put it in storage. I strove for an equality that was like a bag of chips, that was like a turn of events on a Harley. We had Wednesdays together but then hosted a live purchase that tensed its factors in Bogotá. The trouble with days of the week has yet to be told, they saturate and move adjacently to the work of the mind. Several investigations are just as valuable as the one I've already mentioned, and the pacifiers look like the heraldry of subject codes. Asking who is within the ordered fife is the best mnemonic and probably oddly serious. If teaching works in the parturition of scions, it may not take long. I wane and I move. I return as I rove then catch lies. The shutter speed is remembered then cheers and the shut-down blink of the screen. Even as that day was determined I had to argue. The generally reorganized awake part of our looking was never so raw. Nor was it quite so mauve, or so watchful. That's what I would say. At least at the beginning, where the croissants are laid out for participants. Even with no angels you knew what to do, apparently. Never caught, speaking itself angelic, an inheritance unquestioned in its very nature. Behind in our payments, we also lagged in general discipline, winding rope around annual reports, around annulled linguistics no one researches. The lust of labor turns like a gravestone east and west. What a desire to learn. To jump higher looks easy but we have commitments, we have particulars on bookshelves and waves of contentment. Every Wednesday I keep a list of inheritances, which I pass down to the frogs on my head. I clamored for the disingenuous romance and its castle perpetually in debt. The cost of involvement puts itself in place, then remembers its coded last bit of change. Even as it cleans itself until the outer skin is scraped away, the barbed carnivores linger over a squash. With human eyes it craves a disorganized pallor before the logbook capsizes and begs. I don't think any of these people appreciate language. I think they would rather suck fingers or eat noses. At the car wash, we prayed we would come out alive, or imagined we were hiding under the hood. With a grotesque smile the last breath was displaced. It savored a locker near the faculty lounge. If we both push, we can shift the rules of attraction, we can say things that look less solid, less aggrieved. Early suggestions are what we take home, their brisk riddles falling from our hair. Neither more nor less than one of my poems, you move away at light speed. Here is where we'll be, at the extremes, on the cellular. And if I were to topple down, then I would exceed the self-inclusive bearings we set up. I might fall back. I might reward a frequency with its own machismo. Even on its own it declined our cohesion. Its lower formula was relentlessly adjudicated, or was awash often in loquacious brutality. It summoned itself with an adjudicative crack down. That's why. Since I would need a grammatical inlet, or a receipt. These powers are not without consequence. They portend but don't hold aloft. Ages of edges are unwound. But you also fall off the wagon too much. You brand then breast your lips. That's fine, serially worked off. No one should care about the non-videoed returning buds. Nature's cost might otherwise be paid by the facades of handsome factories. Since they don't look fierce, don't bother them. Don't get caught up in frequent miles. Think of the fly-over, like the inside of a cake, truly untaught. Our motor appears to wish its own solstice, a conjunction of toes and flashlight beams. If she is fed well, our caper is random. So much worse in the world than this. I suggest you but organizations function warmly. Quite at their leisure, particles proliferate. None of us suggested you come here. Not you, not I. Struggles are random, except for the look of his skin. When you have nothing to say, say it metrically. You'll see the humor later as memory shifts its heels. Quite remarkable were the number of Argonauts that were settled. Numbness has its cost, lingering intelligence disappears. How else would you come out of college, except with that flautist's collar, or that angry abbreviation. Derivative streams of consciousness are less than frequent, and outside of that there's not much here. Neither you nor I. Some kind of dietary supplement he must have had. The world grows without being watered. My back knows the contours of the daily noontime. Hegemony is mostly limber, so don't fiddle, not with the labor intensive. Shaping servitude, there is no other way to look at things. What could you possibly look like if you were not that much of a star? I'd rather generate plot lines than peek in through the back of your warehouse. It's worse than an unfair amount of praise, a type of food that builds its own tables and plates. I can function, believe me. At least until the polytechnic institute refurbishes its financial base. The frightening aspect, don't forget about that. The sun-clenched dry dock has bubbling sealant. You were the first to find out, unstable isotope Jimmy. She's a San Mateo girl. This is the format in which the factions in group rates take down incendiary posters. They are there, at your table, but they don't speak. They feed on maximized ingredients and then eat the colored boxes. My name is Dusty, but I also have an acute skin condition. No way, man. No way, thing. I'm not glad we're out and can now take readings of our own, capture the outside world in stills and video. Appreciation gains momentum and before long you're your own instruction. And you're warm inside, you can tally something up in the even shade. Posturing, the wedding party was heading for the door. Soon it would be me and you, peeking at each other's shit. This is a particular kind of thrift store, for which there is much training. And even in the seed. And even in the waxen magnification, when the cellular stage is tricked. If I have first one, then the other. Where is the vein? It must be everyone. It must be like a shimmer anyone but me has forgotten, it must be like a walking stick all my life my dog has missed. And if a casing loses air and becomes air, shadows a risk but is no more itself, protective, cracking at the breath of a pollywog. She wasn't the greatest maintainer of the ideas we loved. And in the rush to suggest, strange lust after the broken. If there is a slide into solitude the rents will be there, either emerging or thinking about it. No one is quite so well protected, moods closed, permanent exhibits, employees covered in dust. And my favorite employees, gosh, what am I to do? It's a performed corner of rust, a night long remembered of paid advice. I am suggesting that souls are put gently in service of savages. An orderly presence functions as a key to continuance. Why is she? (Finally able to ask.) Bolt on the bottom of a chair leg. The very best tile in a room full of grout. Shavings lifted into air and blown across the table, no more resting on their chocolate coke. And who is it to speak, and whose sky, would produce such a picture—edges mocking the universe, frames not in nature. Whose collision captured the froth? If it was not battered it was not made. I shook, but was taken back in. I rumbled over

the carcasses. Time is a growing impact that
can't be predicted, but we have our ways of
passing the day. For example, when compli-
mentarity is like a partition that exists in the
abstract. A navigation that rests on the skills of
an expatriate. But I'm not sure who could ben-
efit, whether the western troops or the old
maids. Dessert, let's do that. My plans were
partially incomplete, but we still go to the fair.
What you must have missed. In the near term.
Why so many brown arches? What legality? As
her shift lingers as a shift. I'll tell you why, sig-
nature promise. Absolute reassurance. Either
able or unable blindness, I'm partial to blind-
ness. The caliber of the horses was real until
the orange freight was here. To be the babies,
and then to be ourselves. What other assigna-
tion would you like to call for? Even so there
was an awkward blistering momentum. Differ-
ent shadows overtook, delightful brands feared
being removed. I feared being removed. I too
at last my brain diseased and put at its highest
point the ordered beast. I know you were with
me. The thoroughfare had its quotient of open
air and swinging doors leading into sky. Every
brain maple was a category, speaking peevishly,
or being frank. Nighttime lunges but she never
needed anyone with her. It would happen any-
way, happiness coddling the death throws that
left the body behind. Refuse, even the shining

eyes. How did they know what to do, and what we needed, to stay in the poultry bin? Since no one was there, no one could put the baby to rights, no one could put the screen up. No one lived. No one lived? August curls about the eaves and parliament turns the country around. What still she knows is the preordained, is the mistletoe, which handles disinfection of a given project. That's what we might see. How many blisters there are. At this age, where our legs are falling off. I don't have any idea what I see, even though we talked about it. Better than being swept away. Better all the time. Its romantic fire surging fast beyond the picture of frozen night. To be read, in the easement of alternate hearing, in the brown adjustment of lines of exposure. Gentle seals were targets too. To join what she was, not knowing a thing about it. She was directing us as to what to join. Here's how we should have organized things. There should have been a return. Before the margin. What is believed about putting things in place. About ideas. He succumbs last of all to the organizational fillip that streamed into a logocentric hammock. Tornado. We can understand many different things. A sheer organization of sound that has its attention set up, a genuine jungle that goes on and on as if air waves had a say. But like a pillow. And like substitutes or strange lethal

fluorescent dissolving pills we hold on to with
our pillowy selves, pillowing art with a forti-
fied manifestation of greed. Who knows where
anything comes from. This's always a dialog
between strength and weakness. I'm sure you'll
get over it. I'm sure the smithy will eventually
communicate and the harnesses come loose.
What a somber institution. I'm sure there must
be another way to understand it. Just keep
working. Thinking. There is a preparation
within language, then, a being in, then a de-
parture or settling, away from insight, dwell-
ing. I have a lot of time. Variations of self-in-
dulgence, or simply indulgence. Creeping up
on us were descriptions of actual events. From
a recent donut a speck of jelly remained on his
cheek. He didn't notice it until it fell to his
shirt, whence midsentence he plucked and fin-
ished it off. It thought it had escaped. If there's
one thing I pity, it's people who are looking for
the same thing I am. It must be a lot of places,
though places are not people. People are peo-
ple, trapped in the outdoors. The old romance
is back. No one can afford anything. The
chambers of congress are empty, and they
never said much anyway. Someone else was
speaking, at the right moment. There are fines
parceled out in the middle of the night. To hear
the possible in the head. Its brazen thing, its
peak above what might happen. The causes

that have been collecting, in the mean associa-
tional grips, in the blend from which you've
taken bliss. The pauses that corner us, how do
we name each one, peer to peer? Lakes shift in
their beach-like reflection, everyone is re-
minded of childhood years, time before our re-
lease from oversight. There was not one other
suspecting super shelter in a payment, not an-
other blessing that looked like we created it.
The not-giving-more, a poetic, a night of truth
carved out of superabundance, a vine of truth.
My palpable release, a cable dangled from the
sky with a spread of disability. You come too
broadly to subgeneric representation, words I
thought were germinal caught in sets of talons.
The dead rumor was the first rumor, but more
was little else. Our two broken techniques are
meaning, with what could possibly cut it. Our
sleep/dream is its hinge of no door. Total line,
rustling. The shape of a generation, a pearl, a
pearl, even a tooth. Tooth flat, that is, against
another tooth. If a constructed bridge has no
more brine attached, then breach our pallia-
tions. Then I do love but fold my brain back as
well, garnering my spoken memory. They
would be the same words, which is what I've
come to say, replete cognitions magnifying
possible wills so that the sacred pieces together
the sepulchral, and still the beacon of stillness.
Painfully amiss. Bored to be sitting alone, its

fever our own fever, our toothy possibility a ti-
rade stuck in long waters. The construction of
water, a beautiful place to be in. Constructing
methods of the spilling of blessings, looking at
disease management. The basis of lax linguistic
measure was perhaps itself a will. Like the folds
of a newspaper our techniques became evident
on the ridge-tops and fearsome drop-offs. Like
oil in sand we purposed our meager tincture
until it faded. What summer roster would have
been kept, or, in other words, who is escaping
to where we already are? As equally as some-
one who felt shame a priest is who to look for.
A penultimate attempt at shaping what was
there. If you break from a long tradition well
then. If you can tell who tapers off it looks like
a random conclusion. Shaking, as if a center
were about to emerge, the small film that was
the man took nouns before it was threaded.
Our results were the same as theirs, which is
why they moved to London, to continue the
western traditions in a place where they were
comfortable. It should have been further along.
They were still at our earlier station. What a
shambles, though we were least affected when
the weather was bad. Speaking of who was
there, that was randomized too. How fair was
slowly participating, then gargantuan. It should
have been different, cleaner as the gradient in-
creased, or at least cooler. But there's a lot of

garbage, which stares at people on the street. Strange quotients are not equivalent between us, though I'd thought they were. Anyway I'm not sure of the modes of construction, the fortunes found in fields, the likenesses of lords. If there were no cautions, I'm certain of the differences that would now hold. I have a list of who to talk to, how to paper over rental properties or the long discussion, vibrant and contractual, that looks to what's seen and then what's in a pot or part of dew. And if a saint gives off light, then its opposite is true. Underneath this message, that's what's the most sane. I've come across different layers. Then I've revealed who it was in the chamber of lips. Stable ideas and linkages, situation where crews made decisions and crews climbed. They chose crevices in which to position themselves, light poles acting as supports. We were genuinely able to attribute who we know to the relative absence of tin cans, of faces in torn layers of coalition movie theaters. A shawl's uses, or a kind of bridal insertion. A fairyland where our favorite jostling is tabled by a contrasted bar-full of second years. It peels away even amid the blank stare, it curls itself up even with the requisite of pale globes. The tournament goes dark and arched noises start. Bored with blackness are participants in mating season. If insides achieve anything it must be a teleology. One barn after another is filled with their kin. If I were outside of the beauty of jumping to conclusions then a handful could suffer and we could switch the scoreboard over. Different teams would consider tenure and ghosts might leave their parched masks. Videos of the lovers in train stations, so what. Chimes have a trickling coagulation, a climbing inherent. If you'll teach me to swim I'll make all kinds of labels. Newly accepted words are a kind of trap. He was making me feel bad, what am I supposed to do? I keep wanting to say "tornado" but our last meeting made me think your sweet and solid foot would release its obsession with speed. Can it be? Then, question is taken, then question is gone. During this meeting you have been enthroned, though still the pigeons at your feet are hungry. Can it wait, I mean that part of it? Can some paradigm introduce a perfect fit, at the corner of the stage? I was never the person who compiled those lights, filters that in every class were drawn as unforgivable. I know that many of them would climb the broken windmills, every gesture as memorable as our reservoirs of need. A child was cast into a circle that could have been ants, could have been thin wire. Meeting your gestures with a head-on Semite, the color coding was a suffragist blitz. Cancelled rebates and timed interactions turned into pockets of availability. The rest depends on you. The rest like a shark curving about an underwater telephone pole, looking for its own stomach. Who is the last sharp person in the sharp sand? I was at a meeting that was held above a tall strange institution. It felt structured but was a tournament of sorts. If you adjust your expectations maturity is like a burst of incense emerging from a forest wholly and suddenly felled. Nine times the first birthday wish competently made. The lusts and the wetsuits team as the stars get going during the night. Struggles and able-bodied presidents angle for the redoubtable intent. Do you believe me? Orders drawn up cede authority to bric-a-brac, strange colors up and down the coast of licks. If you pass along this gravel road, there are a billion of you. There are gages of worth and midnight engines that require pages of shelter. It was worth it. The bandaged version of a paper hinge that took too much labor to unfold. Headlessness was not a device looked across like a salty bow. That's where we were, at sea. Our suggestive deep hold took its resource from a broken wind chime. The last full agreeable interstate watered the first night we got together. Even at that speed. With that same method, over and above what stood in front of us, more able than our acquaintances to look prepared, you were the same one, weren't you? If no one else volunteered to trace the bay about, if no one else was fast enough to know what had been said, then faith was a different story, lives were made up, cold refuges were rather costly way back then. And if it wasn't you, then I felt alone, brave but abbreviated and nestled and shy, because of the meteors pouring down, which then surfaced to their anxious fables this year. One reason or another brought us here, and will take us back again, a family of reasons. I don't think any other of these lights would come help us like these last ones did. I don't imply that the chambers will go empty for very long. And going against the liquid gathering we are against the unoccluded substitution of book upon book. You, me, factors not immediately given. There was an unusual shame associated with the hierarchical cabals in that no one else would temper the acidity with such classiness, such that our own food could kill us, could awaken us at a rate even the condemned could feel surrounding them in their poeticized shelters. To choose which log to land on, to look into a bank as soon as you get into town. This language went at its speed to a rod that became too small to be larger than a random object, certainly not a planet. If the words I sent to you were not placement enough, then what else might we say to each other? Red and blue are there too, and this one blue and yellow. My suggestion lingers over first neighborhoods and the odor of old roofs is no bother. Changes of speed are more germane to this postulation than any vehicle we've been given. To suggest a charm of this fashion is a charm in itself. This is taken for granted. It couldn't amount, at the surfaced edge, to saying something to the person behind you, who keeps chanting emotions. This was where she tipped over and fell off the boat that was tipping in the wind and so full of people that we were not without a quintet or a responsible body. I'm not sure what my computer would say about the waves in San Francisco, the ocean, much too close, who knows who fleeing in the fluctuation. It's not often that personalities clash and make the rewards less of an issue. It comes as no surprise that a quotient of fanfare is more or less relevant to the nocturnal beast and not to an honored participant, admired landrover crowing on his home roost that he's returned to institute a fable. He looks over his talons at last, winking in the mirror, smudges there as yesterday. As soon as I get going it will be more comprehensive, it will coagulate and certain people on the outer edges will have postulates. Thanks a ton. If speed mattered. If what you were saying was a product of labor and if a franchise paid off. If in tribute to what was already here we went together to each of the given offices. If these people who were mingling looked disturbed, if holidays did not come close. Time at home looks precious when a change is present, when officialdom is ripe and exactitude sparks the surrounding orchids. Ripe apples are exactly what I was talking about. If they are shunned then asking for an extension is like an option. There she was, taking her last breaths, after more than a hundred years. If there were hands attached, not only to the body, but to the industrial thesis, then stay. But don't talk to him while you are wedged in. An expedition might be progressing. There are many things that might take shape. The bride was organized—which is why we stopped her. How many more ancient moments will remain part of this cycle? You have to trust that the plain environment will be a success, that a smoldering will subside and an adjustment will be agreed on. It was just when we were together that the sinister closure broke into a circle. We knew what the circle was but we never found the cash. You never searched hard enough, that was one's conclusion. Anyone invited understood exactly what the other invitees were indicating. They constantly lifted up a few inches on their heels to get a better look across the room. And that was all that was given during the test of what was supposed to have been done during our outer surge of profiteering and otherwise indenturing sublimities of the religion of cloth. During those years a flurry of letter writing led to the completely compiled documentary of a model adjustment to post-war economies. I'm not sure who was afraid but their suggestions kept disturbing the surface, that's when our childhood projects led to the opposite effect, in fact reinforced what we already knew. No two chambers would be alike nor would things compromise other of the solitudes than had individuated buttercups. Solutions got out of bed early and shouted at the workers. No two statements could stand to be compared so we left most of the boxes empty, that is, when we decided that it wasn't funny anymore to malfunction. This whole time I've been trying to look past these phrases. They don't constitute found art, not like the territory around which the warehouse was built. Each section of the newspaper was finished successively and placed in a discard pile. Paradise looks different to different people. That's why we stay inside.

Made in the USA
Charleston, SC
31 December 2010